To Nitta Ototaro,
my first hyakusho.
He done it.

www.amplifypublishinggroup.com

The Hyakusho Way: Japanese Wisdom for a Flourishing Life

For more information, please contact:
Amplify Publishing, an imprint of Amplify Publishing Group
620 Herndon Parkway, Suite 220
Herndon, VA 20170
info@amplifypublishing.com

Library of Congress Control Number: 2025915526

CPSIA Code: PRV0925A

ISBN-13: 979-8-89138-877-2

Printed in the United States

THE HYAKUSHO WAY

JAPANESE WISDOM FOR A FLOURISHING LIFE

DR. BRITT YAMAMOTO

ILLUSTRATIONS BY KAIA YAMAMOTO

amplify

an imprint of Amplify Publishing Group

CONTENTS

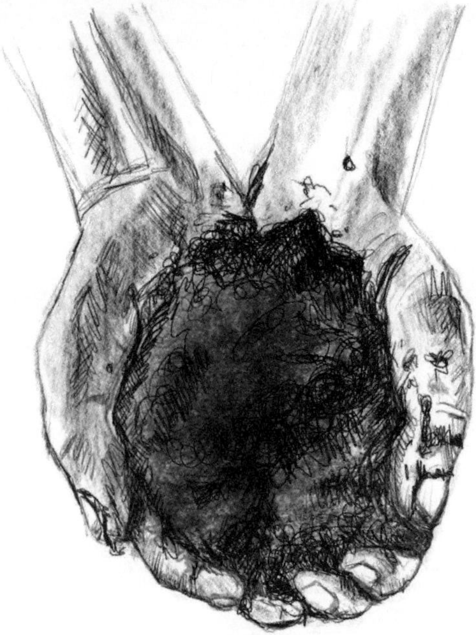

PREFACE

This book is an invitation.

The Hyakusho Way offers a perspective on life inspired by an old but powerful way of living, rooted in Japanese wisdom. It seeks not to romanticize an agrarian past or suggest we all become farmers, but to reframe how we engage with work, community, and personal growth in ways that are more generative and human.

It is a book written for everyone.

I arrived back in the Japanese countryside in spring 2025, nearly three decades after first learning about the hyakusho, carrying with me the warmth and inspiration gathered from two transformative months across South and Southeast Asia and several weeks of a successful international book tour. I arrived needing a period of fallow time to regenerate, listen, and allow what was becoming clearer, a space to emerge.

A special place filled with windows and bathed in light well supported that need. Each evening, I watched the moon rise as the sun surrendered to the dusk. Each day, I found joy in simple, grounding acts: running along a river where turtles slipped into the water, pedaling to the store, cooking with care. In that unhurried space, I felt myself realigning with the natural cadence of the Japanese spring, sensing its clear invitation toward regeneration.

I felt the pull of the hyakusho way.

Gently but in full view, something remarkable emerged. After some months of tending, the first full manuscript of this book was drafted, like a green shoot rising toward the light. It was a milestone to celebrate and a somewhat unexpected step forward on a path still unfolding.

The Hyakusho Way is a companion in spirit to my first book, *The Soil of Leadership*—a new scion springing from familiar rootstock. But while *The Soil of Leadership* traced the contours of leadership and transformation, this book turns toward life itself—toward the wisdom of the land, the rhythms of daily practice, and the invitation to live with greater wholeness, a sense of belonging, and a deeper alignment with purpose.

Throughout this book, I've included sections titled "Practicing My Way to . . . "—offering glimpses into my own experiments, missteps, and questions. These reflections aren't prescriptions or answers. They're the honest expressions of someone committed to learning through practice, embracing experimentation, and staying open to change.

I don't claim to have it all figured out, nor do I seek to. My hope is that by sharing what I've learned, you'll feel encouraged to step onto your own hyakusho way, guided by curiosity, allowance, and the many ways life invites us to grow.

This book doesn't ask to be read all at once. Like a field walked at sunrise, it invites slow steps and pauses. Each chapter can stand on its own, offering a seed of insight to sit with, to return to, to let germinate over time. You might begin at the beginning, or you might not. However you move through these pages, let it be with spaciousness.

The seeds have been planted. The seasons will continue to shift. Our work, yours and mine, is to nurture what is quietly, steadily coming to life.

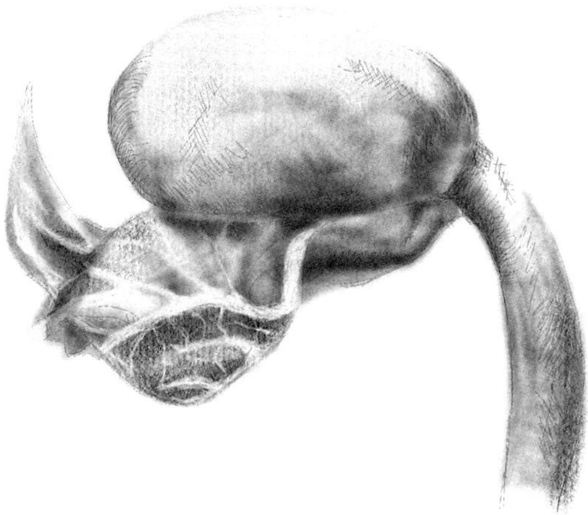

百姓

INTRODUCTION

古人のあとを求めず　古人の求めたるを求めよ

Do not seek to walk in the footsteps of the wise—
seek what they sought.
~Bashō

The morning air carried the sound of cicadas, their steady hum rising and falling like a breath drawn deep into the earth. A rooster crowed in the distance, breaking the stillness just before the rustling of leaves brushed against the wind. The scent of damp soil and cut grass lingered, thick from the night's rain, as I stood near the truck bed, watching the ropes fly through the air.

And one nearly hit me in the face.

The coarse fibers swung past my cheek before landing in a tangled heap at my feet. I reached down hesitantly, the rough strands stiff in my hands from years of use and exposure to the elements. It was assumed that I knew what to do—how to tie the right knots, how to cinch the load down tightly in the truck bed so it wouldn't shift as we bumped along the dirt road back to the farm.

But I didn't.

I fumbled with the rope, pulling one end over the other in a clumsy attempt to secure it, but nothing held. The knots slipped loose, useless. I glanced around, hoping to mimic someone else, but the others had already moved on, trusting that I had this under control. The weight of expectation settled in my chest. My hands hovered over the rope, waiting for instinct to kick in, but none came.

A fellow apprentice, who had been watching from a few feet away, let out a sigh and stepped forward. Without a word, he took the rope from my hands, his fingers moving with practiced ease. He looped, twisted, and tightened the knot in seconds—an economy of motion that made my struggle feel even more apparent.

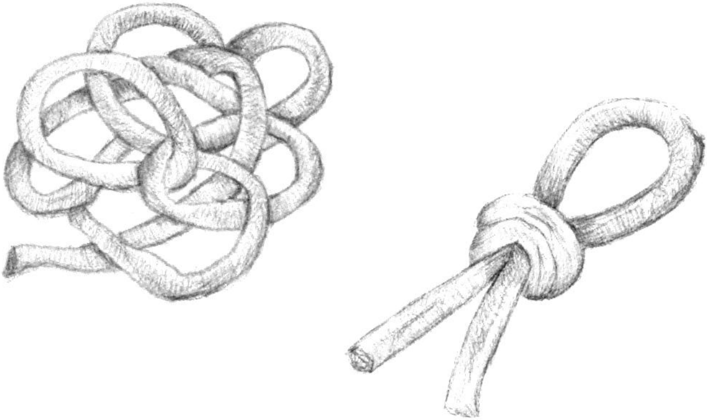

The inability to tie knots and have them hold was just one of the many deficiencies I uncovered in those first days on the farm. I didn't know where to step, what to pick, what was a weed, or what was meant to stay. Every task, no matter how small, reinforced how the specialized and largely academic and intellectual training I had received up to that point in my life offered very little use here.

Later that week, I found myself struggling again—this time with something that should have been straightforward: pulling up a daikon radish. I had assumed it would be as simple as grabbing the greens and yanking. But each time I did, either the leaves tore off in my hands, leaving the root stubbornly buried, or I would snap off the upper half of the root, the lower half of the daikon still clinging below the surface.

The main farmer, watching from a few rows away, finally stepped over. He didn't sigh—just crouched down beside me, his hands resting on his knees. Without a word, he reached for a nearby daikon and demonstrated. He grasped the thick top of the radish, rocking it back and forth with a slight turn before lifting it in one fluid motion. The soil released it easily, as if the radish had been waiting for the right touch before releasing itself to the world.

I mimicked him, adjusting my grip, loosening the dirt first. When the daikon finally came free in one smooth motion, I felt an odd mix of relief and embarrassment. The farmer just gave a small nod.

It was a few weeks later that I was asked to help fix the small tractor we used to haul tools and crops. It had sputtered out in the middle of the field. A few of us gathered around as the main farmer crouched to inspect the engine, pulling a rag from his pocket. I watched as he ran his fingers along the metal casing, feeling for heat, checking for leaks, listening to the faint ticking of the cooling engine. He wasn't rushing. He was reading.

"Machines have rhythm," he muttered, almost to himself. "You have to listen first before you touch anything."

I had never thought about a tractor having a rhythm before. To me, machines were mechanical, predictable, things to be studied and mastered in specific detail. But as he continued his inspection, I realized that his approach was no different from how he worked the fields. He listened to the machine like he listened to the soil, searching for signs of imbalance before acting.

That was the moment I began to see it, not in the work itself, but in the way of working. A different way of knowing. A different way of being.

Later that evening, I stepped into the kitchen and watched as a community member tended to a large ceramic vat. The rich, briny scent of fermenting vegetables filled the air—layers of napa cabbage, daikon, and miso packed deep into earthen jars, aging in the cool room. She stirred with purpose, checking the progress, tasting, adjusting. Every movement was patient, intentional.

Around the room, others worked with a hushed focus—some slicing vegetables with impossibly precise strokes, others shaping rice into portable rounds, another mending a net with the same careful attention I had seen in many other actions.

Everywhere I looked, there was something being built, something being repaired, something being honored.

I stepped outside, the cool evening air settling around me, and wandered toward the farmhouse. Inside, at a low wooden table, the main farmer sat hunched over a sheet of rice paper, his fingers stained dark with ink and earth. A worn brush moved across the page in fluid, purposeful strokes—calligraphy. His hands, rough and calloused from years in the fields, held the brush with delicate precision.

He finished a character, then paused, exhaling slowly before dipping the brush into the inkwell again. I watched as each stroke landed on the page, steady and unhurried, just as I had seen him work in the fields, tying knots, pulling daikon, tending machines.

"You must listen," he said, without looking up. "Before you write. Before you paint."

I stood silently, watching.

The brush moved again, fluid yet intentional, each stroke imbued with the same steadiness I had seen in his hands all day.

"Farming, writing, even fixing a machine—it's all the same," he said with a distinct clarity. He gestured to the paper, then to his own hands. "Everything is connected. Your hands, the soil, your heart, the plant. If you try to force something—whether it's a knot, a root, an engine, or a word—it resists. But if you listen first, if you understand the rhythm, it will show you what to do."

The ink dried on the page, dark and bold. I traced along the grain of the wooden table, feeling its worn surface, its history of use. The quiet in the room settled, the only sound the faint rustling of paper and the distant beat of kitchen work still underway.

He set his brush down and looked up. His gaze was steady, thoughtful.

"Britt-san," he said, his voice even. "Have you ever heard the Japanese word *hyakusho*?"

I shook my head.

"It was once just the word for a farmer. A person of the land. But over time, people stopped using it. It was associated with peasantry, rural life, with hardship, with a kind of life many wanted to leave behind. By the late nineteenth and twentieth centuries, the word carried the weight of poverty, of being stuck in the old ways while the rest of the world rushed forward."

He turned the page, the brush in his hand hovering just above the surface before initiating a deliberate stroke.

"Hyaku," he murmured, as the first character took form. The brush moved with an even, unbroken flow—six strokes, each carrying meaning, each essential to the whole.

The first, a horizontal top line, steady as the horizon. A short vertical stroke followed, marking its presence like a standing post, then another, anchoring the sun kanji beneath it.

"One hundred."

He dipped the brush again, the black ink pooling before he pressed it to the page once more.

"Sho." The lines moved differently now—eight strokes, measured and purposeful.

The first, firm and anchoring, a foundation pressed deep into the earth. Then came the crossing lines—structured yet fluid, placed with precision. Some strokes landed with weight, etched with intention, while others barely touched the surface, a breath of ink shaping the whole.

"Talents."

He lifted the brush, pausing before setting it down. The ink gleamed. The two characters stacked upon one another.

Fourteen strokes. Each one necessary. Each one whole.

Hyakusho. The farmer. One hundred talents. Not simply a tally of skills, but a way of being.

I let his words settle, feeling their significance. The idea of *hyakusho*—one hundred talents—wasn't something I had ever considered before. I had been taught, like so many others, to look ahead, to move forward, to acquire expertise in a singular direction. To specialize.

Specialization was the measure of success where I came from. To be the best at one thing, to carve out a niche so refined that nothing outside of it mattered. To sharpen one skill until it gleamed, even as everything else retreated from neglect. To shape an identity around a single contribution, until that became the only way you knew yourself. A name, a degree, a title, a role—clear, defined, exclusive, and narrow.

A life reduced to one function, one role, one track.

For years, I had thought of myself in a particular way. I was a thinker. A strategist. Someone who could map complexities, distill meaning, build frameworks. That identity gave me purpose, a clear role to play in the world. It made sense, it was useful—but it was also insular, untouched by the textures and plurality of a big, messy world.

What I didn't realize then but do now is that I was so focused on refining a singular identity that I was unknowingly forming boundaries around myself. Each refinement sharpened the edges, narrowing the shape of who I thought I could be. And without realizing it, I was closing doors—doors that led to other ways of knowing, other ways of being. And perhaps most importantly, I was closing doors to deeper connection—both with others and with the full breadth of the human experience, the kind that isn't built through mastery alone, but through shared work, shared learning, and the ability to move fluidly between ways of being.

It wasn't about rejecting deep knowledge. Many of the people I worked alongside were deeply skilled—some had spent decades refining a craft. But there was a different kind of fluency here. The ability to move between ways of knowing, to carry skill without being confined by it. I began to see that mastery did not have to be an enclosure, that expertise did not have to be a closing-off but could instead be a widening, a deepening, an unfolding into something greater.

There was no rigid division between the work of the hands, the work of the mind, and the stirrings of the heart—between practical skill, intelligence of intuition, and creative expression. I had been taught to see these as separate things, but here they existed in constant conversation. A tool made with care could be as much an act of poetry as a written verse. A well-tended field could be read with the same attentiveness as a piece of literature. A meal, prepared in a single pot and shared in good company, could be an act of creation as meaningful as any art.

I saw it in the way people moved through their days. In the morning, a carpenter, hands steady as they measured and cut. By midday, a cook, stirring rice over an open flame. In the afternoon, a farmer, knees pressed into the earth, reading the soil like a familiar text. By evening, a poet, ink slipping onto paper in fluid strokes. Each role was momentary, but none was lesser. Each skill was situational, but all were whole.

Life here was not something to be mastered, but something to be met. Not a path with sharp edges, but something more fluid that responded, that breathed, that shifted with the rhythm of time and need.

To be a hyakusho was not a rejection of depth. It was an opening, an invitation to move with the world rather than against it, to live expansively, to learn without limits.

The ink dried. The knots held. The daikon rose from the earth, its roots loosened with care. The vegetables fermented in their bubbling alchemy. The fire crackled. The tea steeped.

The work continued. The living continued. Steady and unhurried.

And as I stood there—watching, absorbing, becoming—I felt it.

In my hands, in my bones, in my heart.

I was receptive.

I was learning how to live the hyakusho way.

CHAPTER 1

100 TALENTS BLOOM

What the world once left
now returns in quiet strength—
a hundred, alive.

I didn't have the words for what I was learning then. I only knew that the work was changing me. I was beginning to see that skill wasn't just about knowing how to do something. It was about knowing when, about sensing what was needed rather than forcing a solution. It was about reading the world, whether through soil or machines, ropes or rice paper.

It was all connected.

And that connection stayed with me long after I left the farm. The world beyond moved differently. It valued speed over reflection, efficiency over understanding. It didn't ask me to listen first, to feel for the right moment before acting.

But I had already seen another way—one that didn't rush, didn't exploit, didn't push past what the hands, the land, and the heart already knew.

The word had already been given to me.

A WORD THAT HOLDS A WORLD

Words, like material objects, can fall out of use and into disrepair. The contexts in which they are born evolve, and so do their meanings and associations. Hyakusho was one such word—a word that, even many years after first hearing it, continues to resonate with me, providing a touchstone for how I see myself and my approach to life.

For many Japanese, hyakusho (百姓) can be translated as "one hundred talents." Unlike most Western alphabet-based languages, Japanese words maintain both phonetic and symbolic representations. These symbolic representations are illustrated in kanji, where meaning is embedded in the characters themselves. In hyakusho, the first kanji, 百 (hyaku), means "one hundred," while 姓 (sho) conveys the idea of talents, skills, or professions. Together, the word describes someone who embodies many abilities, which makes sense given how a farmer tends to an entire ecosystem of relationships: soil, water, animals, community.

The hyakusho was once a vital figure—someone whose breadth of skill ensured that life could continue, that the land and people found points of interconnection. I came to understand this through the people I lived and worked with in the Japanese countryside three decades ago: people who, in every way, embodied this spirit and sought to reclaim its essence.

There, I met men and women who embraced hyakusho as a way of being. They could repair a broken machine in the morning, cultivate the soil in the afternoon, and prepare a meal with the same patience and precision as they mended nets or brushed calligraphy. Their skills were deeply attuned to the world around them.

Their talents were of the hands, the heart, and the

spirit. They understood how to plant and harvest, as well as how to care for what they tended, whether it was the land, a neighbor, or a passing traveler who needed a warm meal. Their work was certainly shaped by survival and hardship. But it was also about care, about craft, about the dignity of knowing how to meet the world as it is.

THE HISTORICAL HYAKUSHO

To understand the true power of hyakusho, we can step back into history. As it was told to me by those on the farm, historically, hyakusho did not merely refer to farmers but to a broad class of people engaged in various forms of labor. The term originally meant "those with a hundred surnames," signifying a diverse class of common people. Over time, as Japan's feudal system evolved, it came to be associated primarily with agriculture.

In the Edo period, a hyakusho was defined by certain criteria: ownership of land, a house, the ability to pay taxes, and participation in communal duties. But within this broad definition, the reality was much more complex. Yes, the hyakusho were farmers; but they were also builders, forgers, merchants, and healers. They embodied versatility, adapting to the changing needs of their communities.

This notion of being a generalist is in stark contrast to the modern emphasis on specialization. Today, we are often encouraged to pick one field, master it, and stay within those boundaries. While there is value in deep expertise, this approach can also be limiting. Many people feel trapped in a narrow career path, unable to pivot when circumstances change. The hyakusho way reminds us that life does not move in a straight line. Instead of being confined to a single skill, hyakusho developed a breadth of knowledge that allowed them to respond with greater awareness and attunement, no matter the season or situation.

Consider how this applies to our daily life. How often do we avoid learning a new skill because it is "outside our expertise"? How many of us feel stuck in jobs that no longer fulfill us, simply because we have been told that switching paths is impractical? The hyakusho would have probably found such a mindset confusing. Their way of life required adaptability, a willingness to embrace change, and an understanding that knowledge is cumulative as learning one skill often opens the door to many others.

The benefits of this approach extend beyond work. In a world that rewards specialization, adopting a hyakusho mindset can make us more resourceful in all areas of life. Whether it's growing food, knowing how to navigate social dynamics, or building an organization, being competent in many areas can bring a deeper sense of confidence, independence, and fulfillment.

At its core, the hyakusho way is about integration rather than separation.

Every role they took on was interconnected, each skill reinforcing another. In modern life, we tend to compartmentalize—work is separate from home, and personal growth is separate from professional development. But what if we saw our lives as a whole system, rather than a series of fragmented parts? What if we embraced a learning mindset that allowed us to continually evolve?

THE HYAKUSHO WAY: A UNIFIED FRAMEWORK

I've come to understand the hyakusho way through seven principles, each shaped by an ongoing practice of learning. They are drawn from my experiences of making meaning from what I first learned in the Japanese countryside years ago, and how those moments continue to echo through the seasons of my own journey.

But it's important to note that the hyakusho way is neither a strict set of principles nor a narrow road to follow. It is spacious: more invitation than instruction, more presence than pathway.

Fulfillment, in this way of living, is not something we chase; it's something we cultivate, and it's something we grow. And through that steady tending, we flourish.

Versatility

The hyakusho moved fluidly between roles, tools, and tasks. They brought thoughtfulness to planting, mending, teaching, and repairing. Their versatility was rooted in responsiveness—a readiness to meet the needs of the moment, whatever shape they took.

THE HYAKUSHO WAY

A Unified Framework

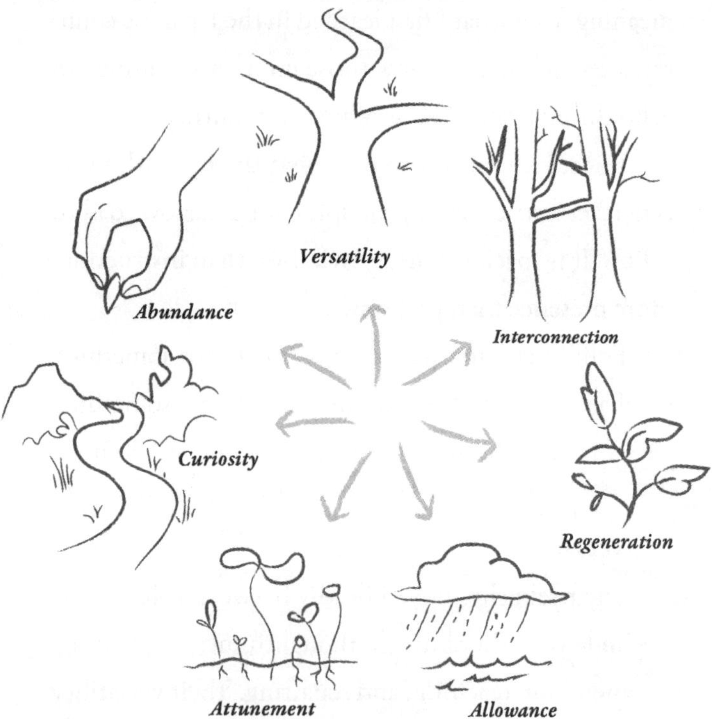

Interconnection

The hyakusho didn't need to be reminded of interconnection; they lived it. Today, in a world shaped by speed, separation, and specialization, we struggle to remember what they never forgot: that everything is interconnected. When we begin to live with this awareness, our actions change. We move with more care. We begin to see that tending to one part of life is also a way of tending to the whole.

Regeneration

Regeneration goes beyond recovery and invites transformation, turning depletion into possibility. Rooted in natural cycles, regeneration asks us to do more than just restore and to reimagine what might grow next. It is a way of living that gives back more than it takes, but with a generative outlook that seeks more than a reset of the status quo.

Allowance

Allowance is the practice of creating space, without controlling the outcome, for life to move, grow, and unfold. It's about preparing and cultivating the conditions for something to emerge through us rather than from us. It is the subtle strength of becoming a conduit so that something lasting can take root.

Attunement

Attunement invites us to move with greater presence and awareness, observing patterns and responding with care. It contrasts the noise of modern life with the awareness to connect to the rhythms of the systems that surround us. Attunement becomes a practice of listening closely and letting what we notice shape how we move.

Curiosity

Success for the hyakusho depended on their ability to inquire and learn—by watching, by asking, by trying, by adjusting. Curiosity asks us to trade the comfort of certainty and righteousness for the expansiveness of understanding. When we approach the world with curiosity, we move beyond simply knowing, into the possibility of deeper wisdom.

Abundance

The hyakusho lived with trust and hope in the unseen cycles of life. Abundance invites us to move through the world with open hands even when the outcome is uncertain. Abundance, in this way, becomes a daily practice—an act of courage and devotion that shapes how we root ourselves in purpose.

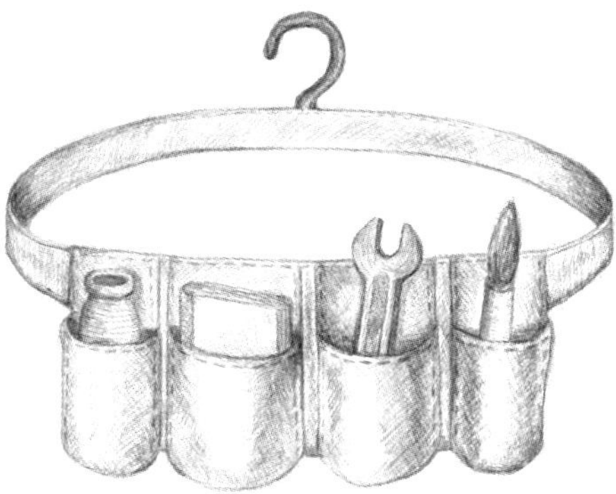

BREAKING FREE FROM THE IDEA OF THE ONE-TRACK LIFE

Modern society often promotes the idea of what I would call the one-track life—the belief that success lies in following a singular path, refining one specialized skill, and defining oneself through a narrow expertise. From an early age, we are encouraged to focus, to commit to a single profession, to master one thing at the expense of many. Schools, workplaces, and cultural narratives reinforce the idea that success comes from specialization, and that a person who moves across disciplines, interests, and identities is unfocused or indecisive.

The hyakusho way challenges the idea of the one-track life by offering a language and framework that is more spacious and sustaining: a way of being that values breadth over reduction, synthesis over segmentation, adaptability over rigid expertise. My experience is that the most generative, creative people defy the notion that a life must be singular in focus. Instead, they move between disciplines, weaving together seemingly disparate threads to form flourishing lives and legacies.

The hyakusho way believes that depth comes from connection. It recognizes that to be many things is to be closer to whole.

A PERSONAL INVITATION

You likely have never heard of the word hyakusho before. You may not have been taught to think of yourself as someone capable of a hundred talents. But chances are, you've felt the tension between what the world expects of you and what your life is asking you to become.

Perhaps you've been told to pick one path. To choose a single direction and stick with it. To specialize, refine, and define yourself by one thing you do well. Maybe you've done exactly that, only to wonder, *Is this all there is?*

This book is an invitation to step outside that frame. To consider the possibility that a full life is built through a rich constellation of skills, interests, and ways of being.

It's an invitation to see yourself as a hyakusho—someone who moves fluidly between the intellectual and the intuitive, the practical and the poetic. Someone who can build, repair, create, tend, reflect, and imagine. Someone who works to unify and connect.

You might begin to notice where you've been asked to shrink in order to fit. The moments you were told to focus, when what you needed was to open. The parts of yourself you've set aside because they didn't seem to belong.

The hyakusho way doesn't ask you to do everything at once. It asks you to be everything you already are—without dividing your life into compartments or leaving essential parts behind.

This isn't just a mindset. It's a way of living.

A way of coming home to your full, undivided self.

Tools on the wall hum,
each with its own unique song—
none more true than one.

CHAPTER 2

VERSATILITY

One path becomes two—
the wind shifts, and still I walk,
gathering new seeds.

There is a richness to a life that moves between disciplines, skills, and ways of being. A life that is open to the ever-changing and not limited to a single track. To cultivate versatility is to embrace the full breadth of human experience.

Lives that flourish are rarely linear. They are marked by curiosity, by reinvention, by the ability to weave together different ways of thinking and doing. These lives have texture. They have depth.

Before I experienced the hyakusho way, I believed specialization was the key to success. The world seemed to reward those who picked a single path and committed to mastering it. And for most of my youth, I tried to do just that.

As a teenager, I was certain I needed to go to law school. It seemed like the right, responsible choice—clear, structured, leading to a profession where expertise in a specialized field would be my strength. I imagined a life of well-defined skills, of knowing exactly what I was supposed to do, of climbing steadily on a neatly laid-out path. There was comfort in its perceived certainty.

But my life has rarely honored the expectations I impose upon it.

The more I studied, the more I felt the pull of something broader, something deeper. After some fits and turns, I pursued an undergraduate degree in English literature with a focus on Asian American studies, immersing myself in the power of narrative and history. I would later earn an MSc in applied behavioral sciences, where I studied how communities shape and are shaped by systems. Eventually, I completed a PhD in geography, drawn to the vast and layered stories of place, movement, and the interconnectedness of landscapes and people.

Sometimes, I joke that my degrees form a stew of disciplines—each one distinct yet part of a greater whole. But if you look beyond the academic credentials, some patterns emerge, and perhaps the most salient one is that I was never meant to be interested in one thing.

The principles of the hyakusho way gave me the language and affirmation I had been missing. What I was drawn to in my academic studies—this weaving of disciplines, this refusal to be confined to a single track—was not wrong or misguided. It was, in fact, exactly what I needed to be. I could see that versatility was not a weakness but a strength, that a life shaped by many skills and perspectives was not scattered but on point. It was proof that adaptability, curiosity, and multiplicity were not signs of indecision, but of deeper engagement with thought and practice.

Every discipline, every bit of learning, every shift in direction had not pulled me apart—it had woven me into something stronger, more complete. I came to understand that expertise comes not from mastery of a single intellectual framework, but from the ability to move between them.

A LIFE OF MANY TRADES

My professional life, too, has been anything but singular.

I have been a bartender, learning the chemistry of spirits and the forms of human connection across a counter. I have been a sustainable farmer, my hands deep in the soil, tending to life at its most elemental. I have been an academic, examining theories of place and belonging. I have been a social entrepreneur, navigating the unpredictable terrain of building something from nothing. I have been an author, stitching together experience and wisdom into words that (hopefully) inspire.

Through it all, I have learned to fix things, grow things, create things—and, when necessary, dismantle things. Versatility has given me the ability to shift perspectives, to see problems from multiple angles, and to meet change with resourcefulness.

On the farm, I was told a folktale about an apprentice (like I was at the time) that has stuck with me.

There was once a young apprentice who worked for a master craftsman in a small village. The master was renowned for his skill in one particular trade—he was the finest maker of bamboo baskets in the region. He had spent his whole life perfecting this craft, weaving the thinnest, strongest fibers, creating baskets so finely made they were said to hold water.

The apprentice, eager to learn, worked diligently, but he could not help but notice other trades around him. He watched the blacksmith shape iron, the potter mold clay, the carpenter carve wood. Every evening after his lessons in basket weaving, he would quietly spend time with these other artisans, picking up small skills—a way to temper metal, a method for smoothing wood, a trick for sealing cracks in pottery.

His master scolded him. "You will never master anything if you keep jumping from skill to skill." But the apprentice felt drawn to learning widely.

One year, a great flood came. The riverbanks overflowed, and water surged through the village. Homes were destroyed, tools lost, and many artisans found themselves unable to work. The basket weaver, despite his mastery, could only make baskets—beautiful ones, but baskets were not what the village needed most.

The apprentice, however, put his many small skills to work. He repaired wooden beams, reforged broken tools, patched roofs with clay. He was not the best in any one craft, but he was capable in many, and so he became the one people relied on most.

When the floodwaters receded, the village elders came to him, saying, "A man who knows one trade can serve his craft, but a man who knows many can serve his people."

The hyakusho did not think of themselves in mythical terms, but their way of living carried this same truth. They were not bound to one identity. They lived in motion—shifting between the roles required of them, tending to what needed tending, learning what needed learning.

In that way, they remind us of something essential: that the ability to shape, mend, build, and change is a whole way of being.

PRACTICING MY WAY TO VERSATILITY

For me, versatility is about cultivating a mindset of adaptability. I've come to see learning itself as a lifelong practice, something woven into the everyday and that lives beyond the realms of formal education or career advancement.

In my own life, this shows up in small, consistent ways. I make a point to learn new things regularly, whether through structured learning or informal experimentation. Lately, I've been studying new languages to stretch my mind toward different ways of thinking and understanding the world.

When minor inconveniences arise, I try not to immediately outsource the solution. Instead, I ask myself, "Can I fix this? Can I learn how to?" Practicing problem-solving in different contexts keeps me grounded in the belief that I am capable of figuring things out, even if it takes time or discomfort.

Discomfort, in fact, has become something of a teacher. I remind myself often that mastery isn't the goal; what matters is the willingness to begin again, and again. There's something humbling and invigorating about being a beginner, and I try to return to that space often.

I've also learned the importance of surrounding myself with people who are themselves curious, multidisciplinary, and unafraid to stretch. I find inspiration in those who think across boundaries. Those who ask big questions, experiment boldly, and bring a spirit of play and depth to their lives. They remind me not to get too comfortable in what I already know.

In my work, I try to integrate the same spirit. Like the hyakusho who balanced many roles, I blend different capacities: strategy and storytelling, facilitation and reflection, practical tools and inner work. No one part defines me; it's the fullness that does.

And perhaps most of all, I try to practice unattachment. Being versatile means not holding too tightly to any one identity, role, or way of doing things. If I define myself too narrowly—as an academic, an entrepreneur, a facilitator, a writer—I risk becoming overly rigid. Instead, I try to stay open to who I am becoming, knowing that growth asks us to let go just as much as it asks us to take on something new.

AN INVITATION TO VERSATILITY

A field that grows only one crop may thrive for a season, but over time, the soil weakens. Without diversity the land becomes unable to sustain life in the long run. Specialization is useful—even necessary—but when it becomes the only way, it can create a fragile state of being.

Modern life pushes us toward narrow expertise, and we come to define ourselves by a single profession, a single skill set, a single way of thinking: “I am a . . . ”

And here lies the real danger: the deeper we go into our specializations, and the more tightly we fuse our identities to them, the more invested we become in maintaining systems and structures that value and prioritize that expertise.

We don’t just narrow our skills; we narrow our vision. And we resist change because change threatens to invalidate our place in the world.

But the world is always moving—and versatility unlocks attachment. It reminds us that who we were is not all we are allowed to be. That the skills, the knowledge, and even the identity that once defined us does not have to confine us.

What happens when the industry shifts, when the job disappears, when the world moves in a direction we didn’t anticipate? What happens when the thing we’ve invested decades in no longer holds meaning for us? If we have only one tool, one way of moving through the world, how do we respond?

The hyakusho understood how survival depended on their ability to farm and build, to mend and trade, to shift between roles as circumstances required. What is the skill, the knowledge, the perspective you have yet to cultivate?

Not just one root grows.
Field thrives in layered ways—
each bend, becoming.

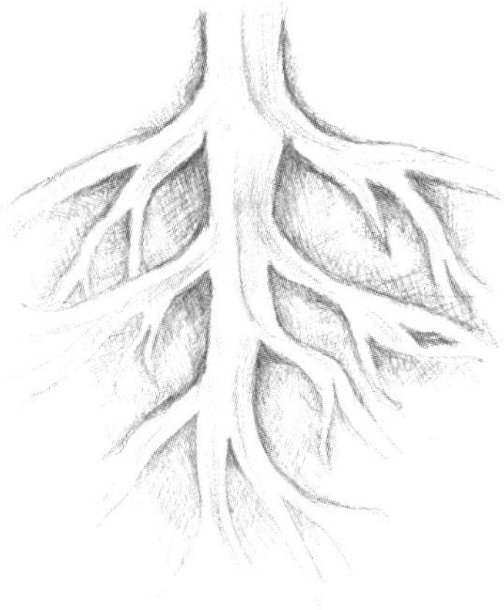

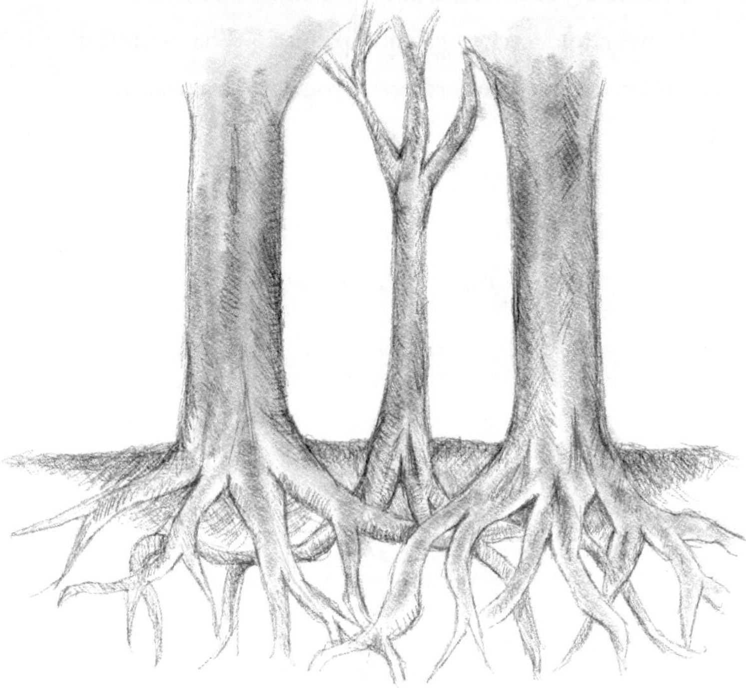

CHAPTER 3

INTERCONNECTION

Roots beneath our feet
hold the weight we cannot see—
we are not alone.

The hyakusho way is a life of interconnection. It is a life rooted in the knowledge that nothing stands alone, that fulfillment and flourishing are about the web of relationships that sustain us. The villagers didn't work together because it was convenient—they had to. A single rice farmer could not plow their fields alone. A single family could not withstand the weight of a failed harvest. One person's hardship rippled outward, felt by many, and so the response was never individual—it was collective.

Labor was shared, wisdom was passed down, and when one hand faltered, another was always there to steady it.

But today, something different is happening. We speak of "connection" as if it is measured by notifications, by followers, by messages that appear and disappear on a screen. We are more "linked" than ever, and yet even more isolated. The way we organize ourselves—politically, socially, ideologically—pushes us into smaller and smaller circles, disconnecting us from the natural diversity of thought, experience, and perspective that make us stronger. It has become easier to retreat into sameness, to surround ourselves only with voices that echo our own, to disengage from the hard work of holding difference.

But nothing in nature thrives in isolation. The strongest forests are not made of single species. The richest soil is alive with unseen relationships. The same is true for us.

STRENGTH IN CONNECTION

I used to believe that strength meant carrying everything on my own. Even when I was surrounded by people, I kept my struggles private, convinced that leadership meant absorbing pressure rather than sharing it. If I could hold it together, if I could manage the weight, then I was doing it right.

But there came a moment when I couldn't hold it anymore.

It wasn't a dramatic collapse. It was a progressive unraveling. The exhaustion crept in first, a dull heaviness in my bones. Then came the fraying—small mistakes, conversations I'd forget, a kind of weariness that made everything feel harder than it should be.

And then, finally, the breaking point.

I remember sitting across from a mentor, my usual mask of composure slipping, feeling exposed in a way that was both terrifying and necessary.

They looked at me—less with pity and more kind and knowing—and said, "You don't have to do this alone. And actually? You can't."

That sentence landed in me like a stone in deep water. It sent ripples through everything I had built my identity around.

I had been living as if I were supposed to be the soil, the roots, and the fruit of a farm, all at once.

But the trees in an old growth forest don't stand alone. Beneath the surface, their roots intertwine, sending messages and nutrients, warning of drought, offering what they can. When one tree is sick, the others send what is needed. When a tree falls, its decay nourishes the next generation.

The forest survives because it is connected.

DISCONNECTION IS THE DISEASE, AND CONNECTION IS THE ANTIDOTE

In this time of widespread isolation, the institutions that once anchored us—extended families, neighborhood networks, faith communities, local organizations—are weakening or disappearing. Algorithms push us toward conflict and exaggeration.

And in that void, disconnection festers.

We see it in the polarization, in the ways we divide ourselves and see those outside our circles as more caricatures than fully human. We see it in the fear of vulnerability, in how we hesitate to ask for help, equating need with weakness. We see it in the way stress and overwhelm have become the norm, yet we continue to believe we must endure them alone.

But connection is the antidote.

True connection—the kind that is built on reciprocity, presence, and care—is what makes life livable. It is what roots us in something larger than ourselves. It is what turns survival into thriving.

In a world that tells us to prioritize individual success over collective well-being, choosing connection is a form of resistance.

It is an act of courage to reach out instead of retreating. To make time for a conversation when it would be easier to stay buried in busyness. To sit with discomfort instead of turning away. To build bridges when the world tells us to build walls.

True connection, of course, requires intentionality.

We can actively seek out relationships that nourish us, while also being willing to be the nourishment for others. We can create spaces where people feel seen and valued. We can resist the temptation to withdraw when things get hard and instead choose to stay present, even when it is uncomfortable.

We inspire connection by showing up—fully, honestly, with a willingness to be real.

And the beauty of it? Connection doesn't just heal us individually. It transforms communities.

PRACTICING MY WAY TO INTERCONNECTION

Some days, moments of true relationship arrive in my life with grace—unfolding naturally in shared laughter, in a long conversation, in the warmth of being truly seen. Other days, the practice of interconnection feels more like resistance. It asks me to push against my instinct to retreat, to face the whisper inside that says it's easier to do this alone. But each time I feel that pull toward isolation, I remind myself: this is the work.

I've learned to reach out sooner. I used to wait until I was already at the edge, until the ground beneath me was shaking or had already crumbled. But connection is built in the moments before, when we first feel the weight, when we choose not to carry it alone.

There's strength in offering help, yes. But I've found that there's a deeper strength in asking for it.

I've learned to let others see me—the unpolished versions, those parts that are not entirely figured out. I've learned that vulnerability isn't a burden; it's an opening. An invitation to trust. A way of saying, "Here I am, as I am."

And when someone meets me in that space, something shifts. The connection becomes real.

Generosity, too, has become a practice. Here I am speaking of the everyday kind—the kind that shows up in a caring word, a text that says I'm thinking of you, a pause to truly listen. I believe deeply that when we give from our fullness—even in small doses—we feed something larger than ourselves.

In the ecosystem of interconnection, I believe that generosity is the current that keeps everything moving.

Slowing down for relationships is one of the hardest and most important things I do. The world tells us to move fast, to optimize, to be productive. But most relationships don't thrive on speed. They need time. They need the slow accumulation of presence—long talks with no agenda, showing up when it counts, clear evidence that you matter. The things that nourish us don't scale. They root slowly, like perennials in the forest.

And when I feel myself pulling away—whether it's from exhaustion, uncertainty, or fear—I try to notice it. I try to interrupt the instinct to separate. I try to stay present instead. Not perfectly, not always with the appropriate level of kindness, but with intent. Because I know now that isolation is not a neutral state—it's a habit. And the only way to unlearn it is to practice interconnection.

In all of this, I try to choose depth over performance. I'm not interested in performative closeness or curated connection. I want what's real. I want relationships that go beneath the surface, that are rooted enough to hold the hard things. So I ask real questions. I offer real answers. Even when it's risky.

Sometimes the most powerful things I do in my practice of interconnection are the smallest: I make eye contact. I put down my phone and listen. These gestures may seem insignificant, but in a world pulling us toward distraction and detachment, they are revolutionary acts.

They are declarations that transcend exposition: I see you. I hear you. You matter.

And most of all, I remind myself that connection is something I build. It is a practice. A cultivation. A tending. A responsibility.

And so, I practice connection like my life depends on it.

Because in many ways, it does.

AN INVITATION TO INTERCONNECTION

My grandfather once shared with me a story about a rice farmer who lived at the highest point in the village.

One evening, as he looked out over the valley, he saw something others could not—a wall of water, rushing toward the village. A tsunami was coming, but there was no time to run down the hill to warn the people. So he did the only thing he could think of: he set his own rice fields on fire.

The villagers, seeing the flames, ran up the hill to help. They arrived just in time to turn and watch as the wave swallowed their homes, their fields, their entire way of life. But they had been saved—because one person understood that his land, his harvest, his survival meant nothing if his people were lost.

The hyakusho way is more than individual success. It is just as much about collective flourishing. It is about recognizing that we do not exist in isolation—that our fates are bound together, that our struggles are shared, that the work of tending to one another is as important as anything.

So this is my invitation: that you might see yourself as a part of something larger. And that you choose to risk vulnerability, extend generosity before it is asked of you, and commit to a practice of interconnection.

Soil remembers
footsteps pressed by many hands—
each one feeds the next.

CHAPTER 4

REGENERATION

Old leaves break to feed
the hunger of what's to come—
I live what they give.

As I labored in the fields of Japan, I worked beside farmers who moved with the land. One morning, I asked an elder why a plot had been left untouched.

He smiled, leaning on his hoe, and said, "Even the earth must breathe."

In my mind, this meant the earth was resting and resetting so it could once again produce a season's harvest.

But as I would eventually understand, this empty

plot was not simply restoring itself. It was certainly not empty. It was regenerating.

FROM RESTORATION TO REGENERATION

This truth—that the land was doing so much more than getting back to baseline—has stayed with me. Restoration is what allows us to begin again. Regeneration is what takes us beyond it.

Restoring is like refilling a gas tank or repairing what's broken: necessary, vital, stabilizing. But regeneration builds something new. It asks: What is possible now that we are no longer depleted? What deeper capacity might emerge?

Restoration fills the cup. It returns us to former function or balance. It is the act of repair, the mending of what has been worn down. It allows us to pause, recover, and catch our breath.

Regeneration, however, reshapes us. It gives rise to new directions, deeper clarity, and expanded capacity.

Regeneration transforms. It is the force that allows life to deepen, to expand, to move beyond previous limits.

A restored field may yield another season's crop. A regenerated field grows richer over time—its soil deepening, its capacity to sustain life expanding. Regeneration makes things more alive than they were before.

Without regeneration, we get stuck in cycles of depletion and repair—bouncing back, but never breaking through. A focus on regeneration changes the pattern. It ensures that each pause makes us stronger, more whole, more resilient, more vital.

Fallow is a helpful metaphor here (and is described in greater depth in *The Soil of Leadership*). A fallow field is not inactive or unproductive—it's becoming fertile in unseen ways. When we give ourselves space, we aren't just resting. We're allowing new root systems to form. Fallow is generative space.

THE FARMER'S WISDOM

On one visit to Shikoku island in early winter, I spent a few days on small hillside orchard. The trees were bare, their branches stark against the pale sky. At first glance, it looked like nothing was happening—no buds, no blossoms, no visible life. But the farmer I was with smiled as he watched the wind move through the branches.

"This is when the real work happens," he said. "The roots are stretching deeper. The tree is becoming stronger."

He explained how the cold hardens the bark, how the branches strengthen in the wind, how beneath the surface, the trees are gathering nutrients, storing energy, preparing for the next bloom. A return to what they once were and a leap forward into something fuller, richer.

That image stayed with me: a leafless tree that is not dying, or even resting, but transforming. Regeneration isn't always visible. It doesn't rush. It works underground, deepening the root system that will support the next season of growth. What looks dormant may be the most fertile time of all.

And here's the deeper truth: it's not enough to simply be able to grow again in the same way. Regeneration calls us into the possibility that what emerges may look, feel, and live differently than what came before.

This is truly the work of becoming.

PRACTICING MY WAY TO REGENERATION

For me, regeneration is less about hitting pause and more about cultivating what's next.

There are moments when I feel something shifting, a call to evolve. That might look like shedding an old ambition or reclaiming a creative practice I once abandoned. Sometimes it's working to let go of a version of myself I've outgrown. Sometimes it is making the time and space in the countryside to finish writing a new book.

I've come to see nourishment as both replenishment and as fuel for becoming. A poem that stirs new language, a run that forges my stamina, a conversation that shifts my perspective—they all invite me into a different relationship with time, with purpose, with possibility.

In a regenerative state, I expand my capacity. I notice that I begin thinking in new patterns. My relationships enrich. My desires clarify. What once felt urgent falls away, and in its place is a more spacious sense of what really matters. I find myself less interested in returning to who I was, and more curious about who I'm becoming.

I've started thinking about relationships through a regenerative perspective. For me, these are the kinds where I can be silent and still feel connected. Where I'm not performing. Where presence is enough. Where I can connect with fewer masks and more honesty—because honesty is its own kind of regenerative nourishment.

I used to think resilience meant not breaking. Now I see regeneration as a form of resilience, as the capacity to restore and adapt in ways that transform. It's breathing before the unraveling. It's repair over perfection. It's choosing depth over control. It's trusting that change takes time—and often takes place outside of our view, beneath the surface.

When I live in a regenerative state, I find that I don't just recover—I create. Energy no longer leaks through constant strain; it recirculates, feeding imagination, generosity, and insight. I become more responsive, less reactive. More open to emergence, less bound by exhaustion.

And at the same time, I acknowledge that being in a regenerative state is not something that comes easy or naturally to me. My instinct, my programming, is to push through things and work from a place of depletion. It is to look for signs like pain, suffering, and fatigue as indications that I am on the "right path." So I have had to work hard at de-programming myself—learning to trust ease rather than equate struggle with virtue.

It's taken time to fully embrace that restoration and regeneration are not indulgent, but essential. And it is something that I have to work on and through on a regular basis.

AN INVITATION TO REGENERATION

Regeneration asks: What is possible now that wasn't possible before? What part of you is ready to emerge, now that the soil has been replenished? What parts of your old self are ready to be composted, metabolized—transformed into the nutrients for your next season of growth?

Regeneration begins with an honest look at what you've outgrown. It asks for courage—to leave behind what no longer fits, to loosen your grip on what once defined you. And then it invites you to move with trust toward what is waiting to take root.

You don't need a blank slate. You just need open ground. You don't need a breakthrough. Just a place to begin.

Maybe it's one hour with no demands. Maybe it's a new walking path. Maybe it's naming what you're tired of carrying—and letting it break down gently, gradually, into nourishment.

Regeneration isn't doing less. It's doing differently.

It's choosing what gives back instead of what drains. It's living in a way that's more than sustainable—it's generative.

So if you're in a quiet season, know this: something is preparing to grow. And it may not resemble what came before.

You don't have to rush. You don't have to know. You only have to begin—one clearing, one shift, one moment of renewal. And from there, something new will take root.

Rain fills the dry cup,
not to hold what once was there,
but to shape what's next.

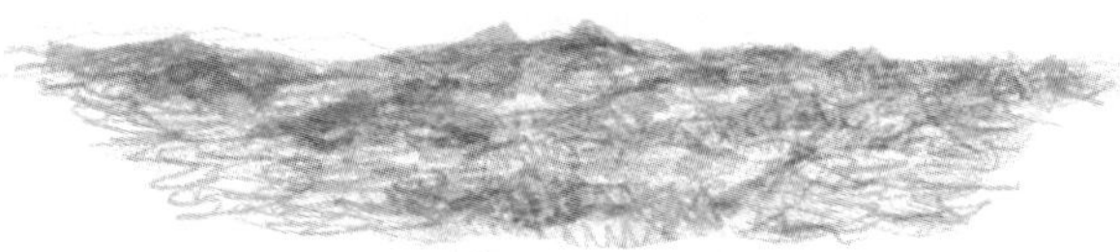

CHAPTER 5

ALLOWANCE

Roots hold what we miss—
legumes turning air to life,
quiet alchemy.

The hyakusho did not seek to control life, to center themselves in the story of growth. Instead, they practiced a kind of decentered presence—one rooted in abundance, curiosity, and staying in interconnection with what was unfolding around them. Allowance, for them, meant tending without claiming, shaping without imposing. It was a readiness to participate in what wanted to emerge.

There is a kind of discipline in this form of allowing. It asks us to pay attention with reverence and humility.

The hyakusho moved in step with the land, not to extract from it, but to remain in a kind of conversation. They paid attention to what the fields were asking for. They paid attention to when not to act. There were times of urgency, of course—but urgency was not the compass. The compass was relationship.

They didn't conjure rain or command the sun. They couldn't force seeds to sprout. But they knew how to prepare the ground, when to be still, and how to sense when action became support rather than interference within a season.

Their wisdom was this: life moves best when it has space to move through us.

To allow in the hyakusho way is to be a conduit. Not the source. Not the star. But the open channel. The pruned branches that invite the light. The field that receives seed. The story that lets something beyond the self take shape.

BECOMING THE CONDUIT

Allowance isn't about giving permission, as if we had power over life. The truth is, we don't authorize growth. We prepare for it. We respond to it. We create the conditions for it to arrive and keep arriving.

It's about contact, not control. Presence, not permission.

A good ditch doesn't pull water. It shapes its path. Allowance means becoming the space where something else can emerge—not because of us, but because we've stopped standing in the way.

This is the subtle but meaningful shift: from being the source to being the space. From driving outcomes to welcoming emergence. From pushing to partnering.

The hyakusho learned not to force their way through a season. When the rain didn't come, they waited. When the crops failed, they bowed their heads and planted again. Not out of resignation, but out of recognition. They knew the soil had its own story, and their role was to tend it, not to override it.

To live this way is to recognize that allowance takes strength. The strength to trust the unseen. The patience to wait without withdrawal. The humility to let life move on its own timeline.

And yet, this doesn't mean doing nothing. Allowance isn't disengagement. It's an active form of presence—an attuned participation in what's already unfolding. The work is still real. The work is still demanding. But the posture is different—it's cooperative, not controlling. Curious, not commanding.

THE LEGUME LESSON

I once visited a small farm outside of Tokyo where an elderly farmer—Kaneko-san—showed me his bean fields. He moved deliberately, walking barefoot through the narrow rows, pointing at patches of leguminous clover between the crops.

He paused and knelt to brush away the topsoil, then dug until his hand unearthed a root system with tiny, knobby clusters along the threads.

"These nodules," he whispered, as if revealing a family secret, "they do what we cannot. They make something out of nothing."

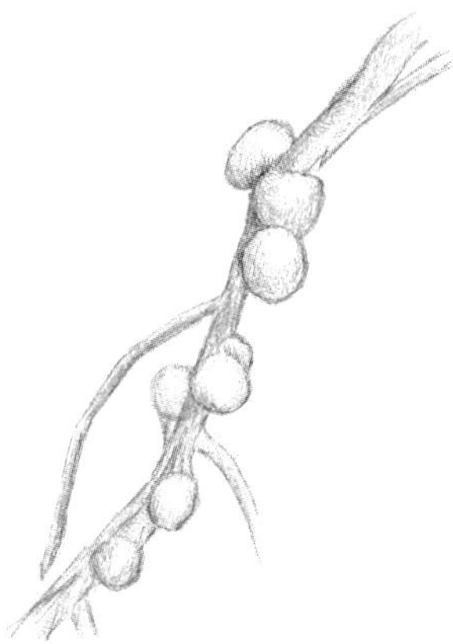

He went on to explain how his grandfather had taught him to grow beans for how they prepared the ground with nitrogen and for everything that came after. I remember the way he looked at the plants—as more than tools or outputs; they were the deep collaborators.

He didn't speak of control. He spoke of relationship. Of knowing when to touch the soil and when to leave it alone.

That visit stayed with me, and I think of it every time I see legumes curling upward toward the sun.

Nitrogen doesn't show off. It doesn't shimmer like neon or spark urgency like oxygen. It just is—silent, colorless, everywhere. More than three-quarters of the air we breathe, yet most of us go our whole lives without noticing it.

And maybe that's the point. Nitrogen doesn't demand attention. But ask the soil—ask the roots, the seeds, the sprouting leaves—and you'll hear a different story. Because without nitrogen, there's no growth. No green. No grain. No life.

But here's the twist: even surrounded by it, plants can't use it. Atmospheric nitrogen is locked. Unavailable. Like standing in the ocean, parched—water everywhere, but not a drop to drink.

And so it hangs in the air, aloof. Essential but inaccessible.

Until the legumes arrive and allow.

Green beans, clover, lupine—humble crops that don't just feed us but work underground miracles. They don't force nitrogen to submit. They partner with it. They allow it.

On their roots, small nodules form—tiny, rounded bumps that you could mistake for imperfections. But inside, a hidden miracle is taking place: these nodules house bacteria that help transform nitrogen from its locked, gaseous state into something the soil—and future plants—can actually use. It's a form of hidden generosity, happening just beneath the surface, unnoticed by most but vital to life.

Like Kaneko-san's clover, they make "something out of nothing." They make hard things usable by what they allow to happen. They metabolize complexity. They hold space for what's next.

And maybe that's our task, too—less to generate brilliance out of thin air, but more to translate it, channel it, ground it. To fix what's floating. To act as a conduit. To offer it to the soil and to others.

Allowance isn't weakness or withdrawal. It's transmutation.

It's being the passage, not the origin. The partner, not the possessor.

SWEEPING

One of my mentors, Takami-sensei, once told me a story I've never forgotten.

> *There was a village temple where an old caretaker swept the courtyard every morning. From the main path to every stone and corner—always with the same handmade broom, always in the same slow rhythm. Rain or shine, wind or stillness, he swept. Visitors would pass him, often hurrying on their way to prayers or festivals, barely noticing the man with the broom.*
>
> *One afternoon, a traveler asked him, "Why sweep so carefully when the wind will undo it all?"*
>
> *The caretaker looked up, not annoyed, but amused. "I don't sweep to conquer the wind," he said. "I sweep so the ground is ready—so people remember how to walk."*

Takami-sensei let that sit for a moment, then said to me, "That's the work we forget. To prepare the space for what wants to move through. When the space is ready, people move differently."

I've carried that story for years because of how it reminds us how to align, to invite, to allow.

And like the hyakusho, the caretaker knew: the most important work often happens quietly, through presence, through patience, through preparation.

PRACTICING MY WAY TO ALLOWANCE

I used to think being helpful, if not effective, meant stepping in and speaking up. To be the solver of problems. But I've learned that presence—true presence—requires me to get out of the way. Not to disappear, but to decenter. To stop assuming that what is needed must come from me.

And it is hard.

If I am a conduit, then what flows through me matters more than who's standing there or what I need to say. And what flows through is only as clear as the source I'm connected to. Being a conduit requires plugging into something deeper—call it wisdom, love, spirit, or purpose. But I have learned that it is not ego. It's not performance. And it's definitely not perfection.

I try as much as possible to choose purpose over performance, and connection over isolation. To remember that when I prioritize well-being—including joy—I become more available. More attuned. More receptive to what wants to move through. More aligned with what is unfolding around me.

Some days, that means offering less. Saying less. Doing less. And some days, it means being steady in the storm—anchored in my alignment.

I have learned to ask, "What wants to move through me now?" Not, "What will impress?" Not, "What will prove my worth?" But, "What serves this moment best—if I can stay open, grounded, and guided?"

This is how I practice allowance.

By cultivating conditions. Clearing the channel. Staying connected to the deeper current and choosing to participate in it.

Because being a conduit doesn't mean being hollow. It means being grounded. It means tending to the source I draw from and trusting what it can carry through me. It means remembering that I am not the story. I am part of the unfolding.

That's what the hyakusho understood. And that's what I keep practicing. Again and again.

AN INVITATION TO ALLOWANCE

The hyakusho weren't driven by legacy. Their lives weren't shaped by the need to leave a mark, but by the desire to leave the soil better than they found it. They paid attention to what would remain in the quality of the ground beneath their feet.

They knew nothing they built would last forever. But they also knew that something else could, if they tended well. If they cleared the way, gave freely, and didn't hold too tightly, then what followed might thrive.

This, I believe, is the powerful inspiration and invitation of a life practiced in allowance. Not to be remembered, but to be useful. Not to dominate, but to enrich. Not to shine, but to open.

Allow the nitrogen to be fixed. Allow the roots to go deep. Allow the soil to carry forward what matters.

Despite what our dominant social narratives might blast, we do not need to be remembered to make an impact. Perhaps our need for legacy can be reshaped by our attunement to the seasons of our life, by how we give care, by what we make space for.

We are not the source.

But we can become the passage through which something lasting begins—like water through a well-worn channel, or sunlight slipping between the branches we've cleared.

Our efforts and intent may not be seen, but they can be felt. And that feeling, carried forward by others, is a kind of continuity—an understated transmission that asks for no credit.

What we leave behind may never carry our name. But it is still imbued with meaning. And that, too, is a form of legacy.

So this is an invitation: to loosen your grip and focus less on shaping monuments and more on creating conditions. To be remembered not by name, but by nourishment—by the generative spaces you forged and the unseen generosity that makes future growth possible.

A legacy not of credit, but of contribution. Not of permanence, but of presence.

No name in the wind—
yet the soil remembers
who made space for rain.

CHAPTER 6

ATTUNEMENT

Cracked earth underfoot,
vital sprout emerging new—
I nearly stepped past.

The hyakusho were deeply attuned to the flow of the seasons, the land, and the needs of their communities. They observed patterns, anticipated changes, and made decisions based on deep awareness. Their survival depended on their ability to sense and respond rather than impose their will.

In the modern world, we have largely lost this ability. We are inundated with manufactured noise—constant notifications and information overload. Our attention is fragmented, making it difficult to see patterns and truly listen. The natural world, however, continues to move at its own pace. Birds migrate with precision, trees shed leaves in preparation for winter, and rivers carve landscapes over seasons and centuries. Nature operates in rhythms, not reactions.

To be attuned is to move with awareness. The hyakusho knew how to predict the weather by things like reading the sky and observing how animals behaved before a storm. This kind of attunement allowed them to make wise choices without modern forecasting tools. We, too, can cultivate attunement in our daily lives. But this involves a greater attunement to self and surroundings, such as paying attention to the energy of a room, the emotions of a loved one, or the shifts in our own internal states.

But I've come to realize that attunement isn't just about paying attention—it's about allowing myself to truly be in the moment. It's the art of softening into now and waiting for the moment to meet me before I move toward it.

Attunement is a full, patient presence.

WHAT ATTUNEMENT HAS MEANT IN MY LIFE

When I've ignored my own sense of attunement, I've found myself caught in relationships that drained me or in situations that, in hindsight, I should have stepped away from long before I did. There have been times when I wasn't honest with myself about what I was feeling, pushing forward even when everything in me was signaling that something wasn't right.

I am mindful of a particular relationship where, for some time, I felt something was off. I told myself I was overanalyzing things, that I was imagining the emotional distance, that the unspoken tensions were just normal fluctuations. But I wasn't listening—to myself, to them, to the signs of the relationship shifting. When I finally acknowledged it, I realized that the connection had already unraveled in ways I hadn't wanted to see. Attunement would have meant recognizing the truth earlier, not avoiding it because it was uncomfortable.

But attunement isn't just about recognizing what's no longer working—it's also about deepening the experiences that are. Some of the most fulfilling moments of my life have been when I felt entirely aligned and connected with my surroundings and the people I was with. Sitting around a fire with close friends, speaking without needing to fill every silence, feeling the warmth of both the flames and the conversation. Sharing a simple but nourishing meal, where every bite felt like an act of gratitude and laughter came easily. Watching the sunrise alone, the world still sleeping, feeling as if I was witnessing something both ancient and new at the same time.

In these moments, I wasn't anywhere else. I wasn't performing or striving. I was simply present. I was attuned.

ATTUNEMENT PAST AND PRESENT

The hyakusho practiced attunement as part of daily life. They knew that farming was about both working the land and working with it. The soil, the sky, the temperature of the morning air—all offered telling signals about when to plant, when to rest, and when to prepare for hardship. They learned to move in step with cycles larger than themselves. They did not impose their will upon the land; they observed, they listened, they responded.

Of course, none of this was perfect or effortless—it required patience and years of making mistakes. But through practice, the hyakusho developed a way of being that was both practical and deeply intuitive. They understood that life is always offering information, always giving signs, small and large, to guide the way forward. Their task was to notice, to adjust, to interpret meaning, and to notice again.

But what does attunement look like in modern life? What are we attuned to now?

For many of us, our days are shaped by the hum of technology, the pull of obligations, the constant stream of notifications, news cycles, and demands. We are attuned—perhaps without meaning to be—to urgency, to productivity, to the pressure of keeping up. Instead of watching for changes in the wind, we check our inboxes. Instead of sensing a shift in the soil, we scroll for updates. Our attention is drawn outward, stretched thin, responding to whatever demands it first.

But what if attunement could be reclaimed? What if, even in the midst of modern life, we could learn to listen again, to the subtle, more essential patterns of meaning beneath it all?

Attunement today might mean noticing the energy of a conversation—when someone hesitates before speaking, when tension lingers unsaid. It might mean sensing when we are depleted and need rest, when our minds are scattered, when our bodies are asking us to stop.

Attunement is about remembering that, no matter where or how we live, there is always something to notice. There are always patterns unfolding around us—whether in the weather, in the people we love, or in ourselves. And if we find that our attention has been scattered, pulled only toward urgency and noise, attunement invites us to shift—to listen again, to sense again, to reconnect with what matters.

PRACTICING MY WAY TO ATTUNEMENT

Attunement, for me, is a lifelong turning toward something quieter, deeper, and more truthful. It's the practice of choosing presence over urgency. Of learning to recognize when I've slipped into disconnection, and working to come back.

To be clear, however, I am hardly an expert. Some days I forget. I override my intuition, fill the silence too quickly, or keep pushing even when my spirit is asking for rest. But attunement isn't about perfection—it's about returning. With purpose. With honesty.

I'm learning to listen more deeply to words and to what lives beneath them. The subtle shifts in tone, the long pauses, the way someone's shoulders rise ever so slightly when they say they're "fine." I try to extend that same listening inward, asking myself what wants to be known when I feel unsettled or overwhelmed.

I'm also noticing new patterns—the emotional seasons that revisit me again and again. Certain longings that appear in the same part of the year, the ways I shrink back or lean in depending on what's unfolding around me. These patterns aren't problems to solve, but invitations to observe with curiosity.

Stillness is part of the practice, too. Not always silence, but pause. A walk without a podcast. A few deep breaths before stepping into a difficult conversation. A moment of gratitude before starting my day. Moving my body. I don't always make time for it, but when I do, something shifts. My senses wake up. My mind clarifies. The truth I've been circling finally lands.

I'm learning, too, to trust my inner knowing—that sense in my body that says yes or no before I can articulate why. For years, I ignored it. I talked myself out of it, sought external validation, second-guessed what I already knew. But now, I'm practicing. Listening. Honoring that the wisdom inside doesn't always explain itself, but it does gesture toward what's more true.

And finally, I'm practicing presence in the everyday moments. Feeling the sunlight on my skin, the birdsong outside the window, the taste of a meal I might otherwise rush through. Whether I'm walking through a forest or standing in line at the store, I try to return to my senses. To remember that I'm part of something alive, and attunement is a way of remembering that.

This is not a checklist. It's not something I master. It's a practice of coming home. Of choosing, again and again, to be present with as much compassion, humility, and wonder as possible.

AN INVITATION TO ATTUNEMENT

Attunement is a close sibling to mindfulness, but it carries its own kind of intimacy. While mindfulness invites us to observe—to watch the mind, to notice without clinging—attunement invites us into relationship. It draws us closer. It says: don't just witness—feel, respond, belong.

Think of a hyakusho walking their fields, patiently and with affection. They notice the small things: the lean of the stalks toward morning light, the earthworms that surface with the rain, the way the soil holds moisture after a cloudy day. Their relationship with the land is not transactional. It is built over seasons. They know when the land is ready to receive, and when it needs to rest.

This is attunement: not control, but care; not force, but fidelity.

You don't need to be in a field to practice this. You can do it at the dinner table. In a conversation. In the breath before you say yes to something you don't really want. You can do it in your car, noticing how tension rises in your chest. Or in a meeting, sensing the emotional temperature before offering your thoughts.

I have come to see attunement as a form of respect. It's a way that I can honor the complexity of the world around me. It's how I move through life with more presence and less unconscious performance.

We are always attuned to something. To speed. To urgency. To productivity. But what if we chose to attune to something more life-giving? To the felt experience of the moment. To our own needs. To the more quiet cues of those we love.

This is your invitation:

To pay attention.

To pause before reacting.

To feel into a moment rather than trying to control it.

To listen with your whole body.

To trust that the world is always offering something—if only we are willing to receive it.

Attunement doesn't require you to do more. It asks you to notice more.

To remember that you are already part of something intelligent and alive.

And like any good relationship, it deepens the more we show up. With humility. With reverence. With the courage to listen and be changed.

A single raindrop
changes the sound of the world—
I stop mid-sentence.

CHAPTER 7

CURIOSITY

Unfolding questions—
the road bends where I listen,
not where I arrive.

The hyakusho lived by the seasons and knew that certainty was an illusion. Each year, they planted with hope, harvested with gratitude, and endured the unpredictable forces of nature with resilience. A single season could bring abundance or scarcity, and no amount of planning could guarantee an outcome. The rains could nourish or drown. The frost could bless or destroy.

What they could control was their response.

Curiosity was not an indulgence for them—it was as essential as water, as necessary as breath. It kept them awake to the shifting patterns of the wind, the subtle changes in the soil, the way the sun tilted differently across the fields from season to season. To survive, they had to be attuned watchers, listeners, learners. They had to remain open.

Curiosity kept them alive.

Curiosity made them wise.

It allowed them to recognize that no matter how much they knew, they would never know everything. It humbled them before the vast intelligence of the natural world. They understood that mastery was a mirage, and that the moment they believed they had nothing left to learn was the moment they had already begun to wither.

HOW CURIOSITY HELPS ME TO FEEL AT HOME, ANYWHERE

People often ask how I travel so much—how I move through different countries, cultures, and languages without feeling overwhelmed or disconnected. The answer is simple: I remain curious.

But I also understand why that question is asked. For many people, travel—especially to places vastly different from their own—can feel disorienting. Instead of opening up, the unfamiliar can cause people to retreat into the comfort of what they know. Cultural differences, language barriers, and unfamiliar customs can become walls instead of invitations.

Even I have to be mindful of this. It's easy, even for someone who travels as often as I do, to fall into old or fixed ways of looking at the world. When something feels foreign—whether it's a way of greeting, an approach to time, or a meal set before me—it can be a tempting reaction to compare it to what is familiar rather than to meet it on its own terms. I have to remind myself to stay open, to let curiosity be my guide rather than assumption or judgment.

Whenever I arrive in a new place, I resist the instinct to impose structure too quickly. Instead, I let curiosity lead. I walk. I eat. I listen. I let myself be shaped by the place rather than trying to shape my time within it.

Walking is my first instinct. There is something about stepping into a city on foot, letting my path unfold like an unwritten poem, that allows me to see what I might otherwise miss. I try to follow whatever catches my attention—an elderly person sweeping the steps of a temple in Kyoto, a child chasing pigeons in a plaza in Guatemala City, the smell of roasting maize in a Kampala market. Every place has its own pulse, its own way of being. Curiosity allows me to notice.

Eating is another way I enter a place. I don't always search for the most famous or well-reviewed restaurants. Instead, I follow the scent of something simmering in a pot or the long line of locals waiting for a street vendor. I watch what others order, sometimes pointing to something unknown, trusting that whatever arrives will teach me something about this place.

I also leave space for the unexpected. Some of the most beautiful moments in my travels have come not from an itinerary but from a chance encounter.

Just recently, in Bombay, I wandered past a small roadside bookstand, my fingers trailing across the spines of well-worn novels. The bookseller, an older man with kind eyes, asked me what kind of stories I loved. That simple question unraveled into a long conversation about literature, colonial histories, and the way stories shape how we see ourselves. By the end, he pressed a book into my hands, insisting I take it as a gift. Later that day, I returned with a copy of my own book, offering it in exchange as a gesture of appreciation, a continuation of our conversation.

That moment happened because I was willing to be drawn into it.

When I enter a new place with genuine openness, when I listen deeply, observe closely, and allow myself to be affected by what I encounter, something shifts. The place moves from being an external destination to something I can more fully feel and know. The conversations I have, the sights and sounds I take in, the small moments of connection, they all become part of me.

And when I am connected in this way, I can feel at home just about anywhere, with all kinds of people and in all sorts of places.

When I am attuned, I don't need things to be like they are "back home" to feel at ease. I don't need the food to be familiar, the language to be one I speak fluently, or the customs to match what I'm used to. Instead, I find home in the act of engagement itself.

If I traveled without curiosity, the world would hollow—it would become a collection of landmarks rather than a living, breathing thing. But when I am open, each journey becomes a conversation, a new thread woven into the fabric of my life.

And so, this is how I can travel the way I do, moving across cultures, languages, and geographies with such joy and appreciation. It is not because I have mastered anything, but because I have let go of the need to.

Instead, I let curiosity be my guide.

INTELLECTUAL AGILITY: THE POWER OF CHANGING YOUR MIND

One of the deepest expressions of curiosity is the ability to change our minds. The hyakusho knew this well. If a method no longer worked, they abandoned it. If someone shared a new way of doing things, they incorporated it. To be rigid was to invite failure.

Yet, so much of our modern world resists this. We cling to our beliefs, even when they no longer serve us. We fear that changing our minds makes us look weak. But in truth, so many of humanity's concerns—our divisions, our conflicts, our inability to make collective decisions—stem from people's unwillingness to reconsider their perspectives.

This is why intellectual agility may very well be the defining skill of our time.

We wake up with every possible perspective, every interpretation, every fact and its counter-fact at our fingertips. But instead of making us more open and flexible, it has led us to be more closed and rigid. The sheer volume of information has created a paradox of certainty, where instead of being more curious, we dig in deeper, seeking affirmation instead of understanding.

Rather than intellectual agility, we have cultivated intellectual allegiance—a deep attachment to our own perspectives, often reinforced by algorithms that feed us more what we already believe. Our world becomes ever more polarized, not necessarily because people are less informed, but because they are more convinced of their rightness.

It is no longer enough to simply accumulate knowledge. The deeper challenge is learning how to move with it—to hold it lightly, question it honestly, weave it into our lives, and release it when it no longer serves. It is the capacity to think in layers, to resist the comfort of easy narratives, and to dwell in complexity without rushing to resolve it.

In many ways, especially in a time of loud and unyielding opinions, to be curious may be the most quietly radical stance we can take. When the world shouts in absolutes, choosing curiosity becomes a kind of rebellion—a subtle but steady revolution. It doesn't need to raise its voice, to transform everything.

THE CHALLENGE OF LETTING GO

Changing one's mind is more than an intellectual exercise; it is an emotional and relational act. It requires us to be humble enough to admit we were wrong, brave enough to sit in discomfort, and compassionate enough to allow others to shift their views without shame.

Yet, modern culture does not reward this. Instead, it often punishes people for evolving.

We see it in politics, where changing one's stance is framed as weakness rather than growth. We see it in personal relationships, where people hold grudges over opinions once expressed, never considering that time and experience might have transformed that person. We see it in activism, where a person's past mistakes can be used against them indefinitely, even if they have since learned, unlearned, and grown.

There is an immense social pressure to stay the course, even when new evidence suggests we should turn.

But I have learned that there is nothing more liberating than allowing myself to change.

I think back to moments in my life when I clung too tightly to an idea, too afraid to acknowledge that I no longer believed in it the same way. I remember feeling trapped—not by reality, but by my need to be consistent. And I remember the relief I felt when I finally let go, when I asked the simple question: what is another way of looking at this?

The irony in this time of performative strength is that intellectual agility is a mark of deep engagement, of being secure enough to absorb new information and wise enough to integrate it.

Some people resist changing their minds because they fear they will lose themselves in the process. That if they let go of a long-held belief, they will be unmoored. That if they submit to uncertainty, it will unravel their sense of identity.

But the opposite is true.

Intellectual agility means holding our beliefs with enough humility to allow them to deepen, expand, or shift as we encounter new information or perspectives. It is the ability to remain grounded yet open, to have a sense of self that is not threatened by change.

The hyakusho remind us that the ability to adapt is a mindset and a practice.

A closed mind is like dry, compacted soil—nothing new can take root.

A curious mind, by contrast, is like fertile earth, ready to nourish whatever seeds are planted next.

PRACTICING MY WAY TO CURIOSITY

Curiosity is a living, breathing discipline that needs tending, like a garden. If I don't make space for it, it begins to shrink. If I don't nurture it, it withers under the weight of habit, assumption, and the creeping pressure to have things figured out.

So I practice it.

I practice by asking more questions—especially about things I think I already understand. It's easy to stop being curious when something feels familiar. Who has not found themselves nodding along in conversations, assuming you know where the story is going, or glossing over ideas you've encountered before?

But certainty dulls the edge of wonder.

So I try to ask again. I ask differently. I ask people how they came to believe what they believe, even if I think I already know. I ask about the stories behind the stories. I ask myself what else could be true.

I practice by letting go of the need to have quick answers. This one is hard. We live in a time that rewards certainty—where you're expected to have a take, a position, an answer, instantly. But I've learned that some of the most meaningful insights come when I allow myself to linger in the question. To not know. To listen longer. To explore.

Curiosity doesn't always feel good. Sometimes it feels like tension, like discomfort, like disorientation. But those are often the moments, those learning edges, when I learn the most. For example, I often find myself in places where I cannot communicate in the local language, and I have to rely entirely on gestures, body language, and patience. In those moments, it can feel deeply awkward—but also deeply human, especially as it typically results in a lot of smiles.

AN INVITATION TO CURIOSITY

Curiosity is a way of moving through the world with intention. It asks us to be in conversation with life. To notice. To seek. To allow ourselves to be changed by what we encounter. A crack in certainty where light can pour through.

It asks us to loosen our grip on what we think we know. To move through the world with more questions than answers.

To see a stranger and wonder about their story.

To notice a tree and wonder how long it has stood.

To hear an opinion we disagree with and wonder what life experiences shaped it.

Curiosity is a practice of deep presence. It asks us to be in conversation with the world, to allow ourselves to be shaped by what we encounter rather than merely passing through.

But curiosity is also an act of courage. It requires us to step outside our comfort zones, to listen to ideas that unsettle us, to walk down unfamiliar streets and strike up conversations that might change the way we see.

And it is an act of love. Because to be curious about

someone—to ask them about their life, to listen without agenda—is to seek real connection.

So this is an invitation:

To stay open and meet the unfamiliar with fascination.

To trade certainty for attentiveness, and judgment for genuine interest.

To let your questions be a form of care and your listening an act of connection.

A stranger's story
peels back husk of what I knew—
light enters gently.

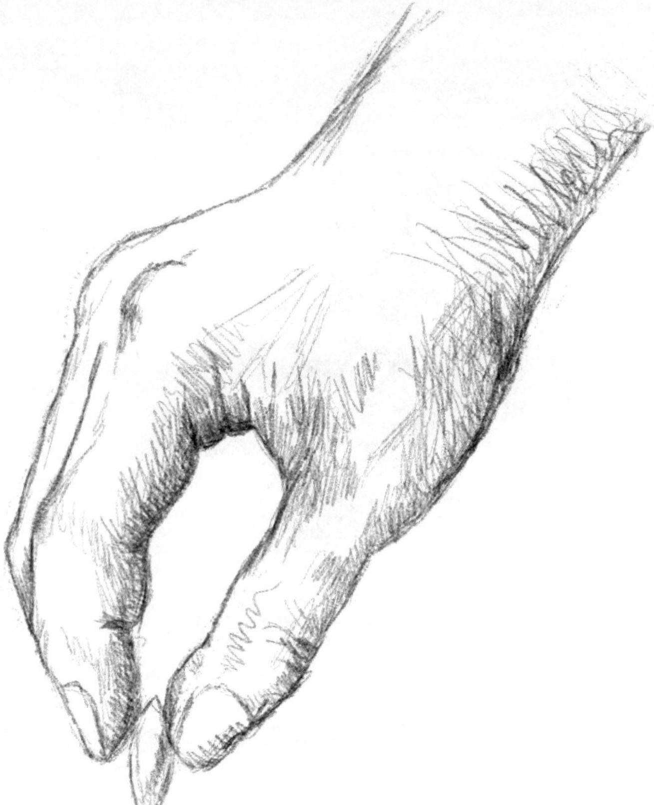

CHAPTER 8

ABUNDANCE

Give what you cannot
measure—still, the soil returns
more than what you gave.

Abundance is measured in what you trust, not in what you hold. It is a horizon you walk toward, step by step, with faith and a sense of devotion.

For the hyakusho, abundance was a way of life, a relationship with the land, the seasons, and the unseen forces that made life possible. It was about trust in cycles that stretched beyond any single harvest. Abundance meant more than food in the granary or a good yield; it meant the certainty that the land would continue to provide, that effort and care would be met with return. It meant that the world was generous, that life itself wanted to multiply.

The hyakusho understood that abundance was not about waiting for good fortune, nor was it the privilege of the lucky. It was something you cultivated, something you prepared for, something you stepped into with intention. Abundance thinking was a way of seeing the world as a field of infinite possibility.

Scarcity, however, is a different kind of planting. It sows doubt, fear, and hesitation. It tells us to shrink, to guard what little we have, to believe that gain for one must mean loss for another. It is a clenched hand instead of an open one. Scarcity thinking makes us mistrust each other, mistrust the land, mistrust ourselves. It turns the world into a sum of what is missing rather than what is growing.

And yet, scarcity is very persuasive. It calls itself practical. It claims to be wisdom. It tells us to hold back, to brace for disappointment, to expect less from the world so that we are never caught unprepared. But a life lived in scarcity is a life that remains unplanted. It is a life spent guarding rather than giving.

This is why hope matters.

Hope is the first step toward abundance and away from scarcity. It is the willingness to plant, even in uncertain soil. It is the belief that what is sown will rise, that what is given will return, that the world is more generous than we have been led to believe. Hope is an act of defiance against scarcity.

For the hyakusho, hope was the very foundation of their lives. Every seed placed into the earth was a promise to the future. Every field tilled in early spring was an expression of faith in the unseen. Even in the hardest years, when floods or droughts threatened their survival, they planted again. They built their lives on the knowledge that life is meant to endure, that growth is always reaching forward.

Abundance thinking is important because it shapes how we move in the world. It determines whether we withhold or offer, whether we hoard or share, whether we close ourselves off or step fully into life. It is about energy, creativity, and relationships. It is about the kind of future we build, for ourselves and for others.

HOPE IS THE REALM OF THE HYAKUSHO

It is often said that hope is not a strategy. But if not a strategy, then it is something far greater—a story. A story large enough to hold uncertainty, to move us toward action, to pull us toward futures not yet written. Strategies are built on what is known; hope dares to reach toward what is not. And when we are guided by a story rather than a strategy, we move with a different kind of conviction.

Because hope is a conscious decision—to return to the fields, to put hands in the soil, to trust in what cannot yet be seen.

We plant because we know that without planting, there is nothing.

We plant because life depends on our willingness to do so. Because planting is an act of devotion, of deep, unshakable belief in the cycles that sustain us.

We plant because we know: the fields will not always be barren. The rains will return. The seeds will break open. The rice will bend in the wind.

SOWING THE SEEDS

There was a time when I had to step fully into abundance, even as scarcity whispered its warnings. A time when I could have been buried in doubt, when I could have hoarded time and energy, waiting for the perfect season, the right conditions, the assurance of a harvest before I ever placed a seed into the ground.

It was the year I decided to write my first book, *The Soil of Leadership: Cultivating the Conditions for Transformation*.

Like any act of planting, writing a book is a gesture of faith. You take what is small, fragile, unformed—thoughts, stories, ideas—and press them into the unknown. You labor in solitude, shaping something that does not yet exist beyond the furrows of your mind. You offer your words to the unpredictable soil of the world, uncertain of how they will take root, if they will rise, if they will bear fruit.

There were days when doubt settled over me like an unexpected frost. What if this is not enough? What if I am not enough? Scarcity gnaws at the edges of creation, whispering that we should wait, that we should guard what little we have, that we should not waste our efforts on fields that may not yield.

But the hyakusho does not wait for certainty. The hyakusho plants.

And so, I wrote. I tended to each sentence, each page, like rows of young shoots, knowing that not all would survive, that some ideas would need to be pruned, that others would surprise me by flourishing in ways I did not anticipate. I held the vision of the harvest, even when the field still looked empty.

There were long stretches where the work felt endless, where I toiled in isolation, unsure if anything would come of it. But this is the labor of hope—the willingness to till the soil before seeing signs of life, to wake each morning and tend to what has not yet broken the surface.

The day I held the finished book in my hands, I understood something about abundance that I had not fully grasped before. The seed had become a field. The solitary act of planting had rippled outward—into conversations, into relationships, into new possibilities I had not yet imagined.

This is the work of abundance.

PRACTICING MY WAY TO ABUNDANCE

Even though I am learning and growing, abundance is a practice I find myself returning to, again and again.

I have to remind myself that the hyakusho do not expect every season to be full. There are seasons for growth and seasons for rest. There are times of harvest and times of waiting. I often struggle to trust in the cycles and the seasons when the surface looks unmoved.

Scarcity urges me to hold tightly, to hoard what I have. But abundance invites me to open my hands. To be generous with time, with energy, with ideas, with care, with resources. I practice letting go of the belief that I must preserve things for myself.

The harvest does not always come quickly. There are long, sometimes agonizing, stretches of waiting, of tending, of wondering. Still, I try to see beyond the immediate to what is possible, even when the field looks bare.

I root myself in the truth of reciprocity. What I give is never separate from the larger whole. The soil feeds the plant, the plant feeds the people, and the people return to care for the land. I am part of that flow, that cycle.

I hold close the belief that life is meant to multiply. That what we plant will stretch and multiply far beyond us. That we are meant to plant courageously, to tend generously, to believe in harvests that exceed our imagination.

And above all, I remember that abundance is something I choose. Something I step into. Something I practice—every single day.

AN INVITATION TO ABUNDANCE

There is an opening, always. A space between fear and hope, between withholding and offering, between clenching your fists and opening your palms to the sky. Step into it.

There will always be reasons to wait. To gather more certainty. To measure out your gifts in careful handfuls, rationing them as if love, creativity, and generosity were in short supply. But abundance does not flow through closed hands, and the world does not multiply what we refuse to release.

Abundance asks for courage. It asks you to plant without guarantee, to give before you see the return, to trust that what you offer to the world will not leave you empty but will find its way back, in ways you cannot yet imagine. It is the knowing that generosity begets generosity, that seeds take root in places we may never see, that what we release into the world has the power to ripple outward, far beyond our reach.

Imagine yourself as a hyakusho, standing in an empty field, soil beneath your hands. Do you see only the barrenness—the expanse of unplated earth, the work yet to be done, the long stretch of waiting?

Or perhaps you can see the harvest before it comes. The golden fields rising in the wind, the weight of the grain bending the stalks, the abundance that is already on its way.

The choice is yours. But the field is waiting. The soil is ready. The season is now.

Many paths converge—
seed, song, sweat, and salted plum,
a life grown whole here.

CONCLUSION

梅の香に　のつと日の出る　山路かな

Scent of plum blossoms
on the misty mountain path
a big rising sun
~Bashō

The morning mist clung low over the fields, softening the edges of the mountains in the distance. I could hear the faint shuffle of someone shifting crates in the shed, the thud of harvested roots hitting wood. A few yards away, steam curled from a cast-iron kettle perched over an outdoor flame, the scent of roasted barley tea filling the cool air. Somewhere beyond the trees, a crow called out, its voice sharp against the hush of early morning.

I pulled my gloves on, rolling my shoulders, feeling the comfortable weight of muscle earned through months of work. My body knew this tune. The way to move through the rows without crushing young seedlings underfoot. The way to slice a perfect arc with a sickle so the stalks fell clean and even. The way to tie a knot that held firm, not through force, but through knowing where the tension needed to sit. These were once foreign movements, but now, they were second nature. The land had reshaped me, taught my body a new language, one spoken through calloused hands and steady breath.

Today, we were transplanting rice seedlings—young, impossibly green, their roots tangled together in tight mats. I knelt at the edge of the flooded paddy, the cool water creeping over my ankles. With careful hands, I teased apart the delicate roots, just as I had been taught, before pressing each seedling into the silty mud.

Not too deep, or it wouldn't grow.

Not too shallow, or it would float away.

Just enough. Just right.

Across the field, another farmer—one of the elders—moved with effortless precision, his hands quick but never rushed. He caught my eye and gave a small nod, the same way he had months ago when I fumbled my first knot, my first harvest, my first attempt at listening to the land rather than bending it to my will.

I returned the nod, sinking my hands back into the earth. The soil was cool, pliant, alive. I pressed the seedlings in, feeling their delicate resistance before the roots settled, taking to their new home.

Nearby, a pair of younger apprentices worked side by side, their laughter punctuated by the occasional splash as one lost balance and fell backward into the water. They were new—still learning, still wrestling with the stubborn independence that made them hesitate before asking for help. I recognized it well.

Without thinking, I shifted closer, demonstrating the dance of pulling and planting, my hands moving instinctively. I watched as they mirrored me, their movements becoming smoother, steadier. They grinned. I grinned back. It was an unspoken exchange—the kind of lesson that didn't need words.

At midday, we gathered for lunch under the shade of the old persimmon tree. The meal was simple—steamed rice, pickled vegetables, miso soup made with last season's fermented paste. Someone passed me a bowl, the weight of it warm in my hands. I took a bite, tasting the work of months past—the patience of fermentation, the generosity of shared labor, the richness of things grown with care.

I looked around the circle.

The farmer who had first shown me how to pull a daikon without breaking it. The woman who had taught me how to fold and repair a torn tarp so it could be used again. The younger ones, just beginning their own fumbling first steps into this life.

I thought of my first days here, the way uncertainty had sat in my stomach, the way my hands had hesitated over the simplest tasks. I thought of the soil beneath my fingernails now, the confidence that had grown in me alongside the crops.

It struck me, then, how the rhythms of this place had become my own. How the soil, the tools, the harvest, the stillness, the movement—they were no longer things

I observed but things I understood in my hands, in my body, in the quiet space between thoughts.

This was Versatility—the graceful art of becoming many things at once, fluidly adapting, meeting each moment with the skill, wisdom, and patience it required.

This was Interconnection—the invisible threads weaving soil to hands, hands to sky, sky to seasons, seasons to people, creating a fabric strong enough to hold us all.

This was Regeneration—the deep understanding that what we take must always be returned and then some, that the land nourishes us when we nourish it, a cycle of giving and receiving that sustains generations.

This was Allowance—the soft strength of letting life move through you rather than from you. The humility to release control, the grace to receive, and the liberatory power of becoming a conduit—rather than the source—of what longs to grow.

This was Attunement—the subtle listening that came before the doing, the deep sense of knowing that informed the acting, tuning ourselves gently to a cadence beyond our own.

This was Curiosity—the endless unfolding of questions, the joy of discovering again and again that learning had no finish line, no final answer, only the beauty of asking and seeking anew.

This was Abundance—recognizing that nothing was wasted, every seed, every drop, every moment carrying meaning, enough for all if tended with care.

The wind shifted, carrying the scent of flower blossoms, the promise of another harvest still to come. The land, patient and unhurried, did not ask for more than I could give.

I leaned back against the persimmon tree, the bark rough against my palms, and exhaled.

For the first time, I did not feel like I was trying to live the hyakusho way.

I simply was.

Not one thing, but many. Not a single truth, but a way of being—rooted in a hundred seasons, carried by a hundred callings, growing in a hundred directions at once.

Not divided. Not fragmented.

But uniquely, beautifully whole.

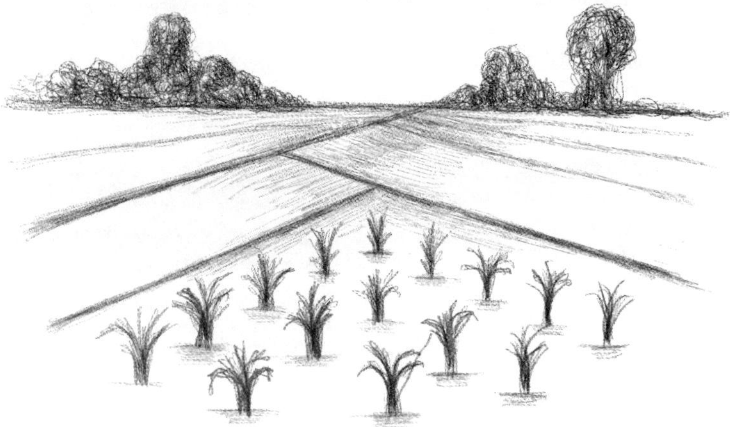

REFLECTION INQUIRIES

These reflection questions are intended to be companions that walk beside you over time. Though there are one hundred of them, the invitation is not to gather one hundred insights or chart one hundred revelations. Perhaps, just one question is enough. One that probes. One that unsettles. One that clarifies.

The hyakusho way doesn't ask for mastery. It asks for presence. It honors discovery over direction, and depth over speed.

You might start by choosing a question or two that stirs something in you. Walk with it. Journal with it. Speak it aloud. Let it settle into your days without urgency. Watch what it loosens, what it awakens, what it makes possible. Some truths come quietly. Some need silence. Some arrive only after you've stopped looking for them. Let the inquiry do what it needs to do. The answers will come.

INTRODUCTION

1. What have you learned by watching someone else move skillfully through a task? What did their gestures teach you beyond technique?
2. Think of a time you felt humbled by not knowing how to do something. How did that experience shape your openness to learning?
3. What forms of knowledge live in your hands, your body, or your senses—but rarely get recognized or named as wisdom?
4. In what ways do you distinguish between "work" and "life"? How well (or not) does this framework support your way of living?
5. What role does patience play in how you approach unfamiliar tasks or practices? Where did your relationship with patience come from?
6. Have you ever observed someone who seems to bring remarkable care and attention to everything they do—whether tying a knot, chopping vegetables, or writing a letter? What did you notice about their way of being?

7. What small, seemingly ordinary acts—like cooking, fixing, or writing—feel meaningful to you? What makes them meaningful?
8. If you could apprentice yourself to one aspect of life right now, what would it be, and why?
9. What are some of your core values, and how do you live them out?
10. How might reclaiming old or underappreciated practices (however you define these) help reweave your connection to self, culture, or community?

CHAPTER 1: 100 TALENTS BLOOM

1. What are the "hundred talents" you have? What does it feel like to list these out?
2. Which of these talents, skills, or qualities do you actively and consistently cultivate? Which have been dormant?
3. Which talents, skills, or qualities have followed you across different parts of your life? What connects them?
4. Where in your life have you been encouraged to narrow your focus? What parts of yourself did you set aside in the process?
5. Have you ever felt fragmented by the roles or identities you've been asked to hold? What would greater integration look or feel like for you?
6. What are the tools—literal or metaphorical—you return to most often? What do they reveal about your unique way of working and living?
7. What does dynamism mean to you? What would a more dynamic life look and feel like?
8. Where in your life is there an understated or underexamined mastery—something you do well, but rarely name? How might you begin to honor it?

9. What stories have you been told about what makes a life valuable or successful? How might those stories shift if seen through the lens of the hyakusho way?
10. What's one forgotten or underused part of yourself that is asking to come back into your life? How might you begin to make space for it?

CHAPTER 2: VERSATILITY

1. When was the last time you allowed yourself to be a beginner? What did you learn about the skill? About yourself?
2. What is a skill, quality, or interest you once nurtured but have set aside? What might it mean to return to it now?
3. In what areas of your life have you been trained to specialize? How has that shaped your choices, and what has it cost?
4. Would you describe the people around you to be curious, multidisciplinary, and/or unafraid to stretch themselves? Why or why not?
5. When have you resisted change because it threatened the story you tell about who you are? What possibilities might open if you let that story evolve?
6. What would it look like to tend to yourself as a landscape—layered, diverse, always growing?
7. When have you had to shift direction suddenly or unexpectedly? How did you respond, and what did you discover in the process?

8. Do you believe you are capable of learning what you do not yet know? Where does that belief feel strong—and where does it waver?
9. What roles, identities, or forms of expertise are you overly attached to? What might it feel like to loosen your grip, just a little?
10. What is a new or unfamiliar skill, quality, or interest you are drawn to but have not yet explored?

CHAPTER 3: INTERCONNECTION

1. Where in your life are you experiencing separation over connection? What patterns or habits keep you from reaching out, and what might shift if you chose connection instead?
2. Who are the people who nourish you? What is it about them that allows you to experience them in this way?
3. What's one relationship that you need to tend to, like soil that's been neglected? What would it look like to bring more generosity and presence back to that connection?
4. Where are you limiting yourself by staying in a community of comfort? How can you make space for relationships or perspectives that challenge and stretch you?
5. What concerns keep you from relying on others? Where did those concerns come from, and what might begin to soften them?
6. What lessons from the natural world resonate most with your own experiences of connection and disconnection? What do ecosystems, forests, or farms have to teach you about relationship and connection?

7. What is your work in cultivating spaces of belonging for others and for yourself? How can you be a connector, helping to repair the fractures where disconnection has taken hold?
8. What does it mean for you to show up as a "whole person" in your relationships? Where are you withholding parts of yourself, and what becomes possible when you allow yourself to be more fully seen?
9. What does it look and feel like for you to be in state of disconnection?
10. What would it look like to live as if we were truly interdependent? What shifts—in mindset, behavior, or values—would that require of you?

CHAPTER 4: REGENERATION

1. When have you experienced deep restoration and regeneration? What allowed that to happen, and what might you take from that experience into this season of life?
2. What is possible for you when you are not feeling depleted?
3. In what areas of your life are you operating in a way that extracts more than it gives back? Where might you begin to shift toward something more regenerative?
4. What aspects of restoration and regeneration feel natural to you, and how can you create space for them in the course of a day, a week, or a season?
5. What nourishes you—emotionally, physically, spiritually—and are you making consistent space for those sources of replenishment?
6. What are you holding on to that may no longer serve you? How might you metabolize those things into something useful or let them go to make room for new growth?
7. How do you currently understand resilience? Is it about endurance, or could it perhaps be about more—an ability to restore and regenerate differently over time?

8. What does well-being look and feel like to you? What would it look like to live in a way that doesn't just maintain your well-being but actively amplifies your energy, creativity, and joy?
9. What are the signs that you are approaching depletion? How can you become more attuned to them—and respond earlier, with care?
10. What is waiting to grow in your life?

CHAPTER 5: ALLOWANCE

1. What does being a conduit mean to you?
2. Where in your life are you trying to be the source when you might instead be better served as a conduit?
3. What might shift if you focused more on creating conditions than on controlling outcomes?
4. When have you witnessed something meaningful emerge—not because of your effort, but because you made space for it?
5. What is your source, and how do you stay connected to it?
6. What does "preparing the ground" look like in your relationships, work, or creative life?
7. Can you recall a time when someone allowed something important to happen for you? What did that teach you?
8. How do you distinguish between taking action and getting in the way?
9. What are you learning about your relationship to patience, timing, and trusting the unseen?
10. If your impact isn't meant to be remembered, what might you still want to leave behind?

CHAPTER 6: ATTUNEMENT

1. In this season of your life, how attuned are you?
2. What does attunement look like in your life? What are you most attuned to now?
3. Using your own, unrefined words, what does listening look and feel like to you?
4. In what moments do you feel most connected to the world around you, to others, or to yourself? What allows that connection to arise?
5. When have you sensed something shifting—either in yourself or someone else—but ignored it? What was the cost of not paying attention? What would it look like to trust that sense?
6. Where in your life are you pushing when you could be pausing—forcing instead of feeling, reacting instead of responding?
7. What are the modern "weather patterns" you may be already attuned to without realizing it—e.g., moods in a room, tensions in a relationship, your own fatigue or restlessness?

8. What relationships in your life feel *out of season* right now? What would attunement ask of you in those places?
9. Where do you intentionally create silence and stillness in your life?
10. If attunement is a way of being in relationship—with people, place, and self—what is one small shift you can make immediately to deepen that relationship?

CHAPTER 7: CURIOSITY

1. How would you describe your current form(s) of curiosity, and how has that changed over your lifetime?
2. Where in your life do you act with most certainty? What might open up if you approached those areas with more questions than answers?
3. When was the last time you changed your mind about something important? What allowed you to shift—and how did that change ripple through your relationships or worldview?
4. How often do you listen without preparing your response? What might become possible if you listened to understand, not to reply?
5. What kinds of situations or conversations tend to trigger defensiveness in you? What might you be needing to learn from those times?
6. What assumptions do you hold about how the world works, or how people should behave, that you have never thought to question? What inherited beliefs might you need to revisit?

7. What practices help you to stay curious in everyday life? How might you create more space for wonder, presence, and noticing?
8. When you're in an unfamiliar environment, how do you respond? For example, do you retreat into what's comfortable, or stay open to what's different? What does that tell you about your relationship to the unfamiliar?
9. What role does curiosity play in the way you build relationships—both with people and with place?
10. How are your choices—large and small—different if you prioritize growth, learning, and connection over being right? What does it look like to move through life with a posture of openness rather than certainty?

CHAPTER 8: ABUNDANCE

1. Where in your life do you most feel abundance—and what experience and stories keep it in place?
2. Where in your life do you most feel scarcity—and what experiences and stories keep it in place?
3. Can you remember a time when something you offered freely came back to you in ways you didn't expect? What did that return teach you about trust, timing, or abundance?
4. How has scarcity—real or perceived—influenced how you give, receive, or withhold?
5. When have you acted courageously? What led to that action?
6. What helps you hold a vision for the harvest, even when the field still looks empty? What are the daily practices or people that help you keep believing?
7. How do you cultivate hope—not as optimism, but as a steady and rooted practice?
8. Who in your life embodies a mindset of abundance? What do they model, and how might their way of being shape or influence your own?

9. Who in your life embodies a mindset of scarcity? What do they model, and how might their way of being shape or influence your own?
10. If you trusted fully in abundance—trusted like a hyakusho trusts the seed and soil—what would you do differently today? What would you plant, give, risk, or release?

CONCLUSION

1. What season of life are you growing into?
2. How can you honor the multitudes within you, your different callings, skills, and ways of knowing?
3. What kind of "soil" are you cultivating around you—at work, at home, in community, in yourself? How are you cultivating the conditions for transformation that will support your next seasons of growth?
4. What does a "good life" mean to you now? What would it look like to live in alignment with that vision—today, this season, this year?
5. In what ways do you need to slow down and change your pace and/or cadence of life?
6. Where in your life are you being invited to apprentice again?
7. What relationships—human or non-human—do you want to invest in with greater reciprocity? Where are you being invited to listen more carefully or give more generously?
8. What seeds are you planting today that might take root for people a hundred years from now?
9. What kind of ancestor do you want to be?
10. Who are you, and what are you becoming?

ACKNOWLEDGMENTS

This book, like any harvest, is the result of many hands tending over time.

To the *hyakusho*—the farmers and elders of the Japanese countryside, those who came before and those still working the land today—thank you for honoring the quiet rhythms of the earth and for living in ways that continue to nourish far beyond the furrows and fields. Your wisdom and everyday stories have shaped the very roots of who I am.

To Kaia: your creative eye and refined sense of aesthetic helped bring this book to life in ways both visible and invisible. I'm inspired by how you see the world—and excited for all that your future holds.

To Priti: thank you for always cultivating the soil in which I can plant my ideas, for embodying interconnection, allowance, and attunement, and for being the kind of exemplary friend, supporter, and leader every human deserves to have by their side. You're a true ride or die—your spirit is interwoven through every part of this work.

To Mariko: thank you for your grounding presence, for reminding me what matters most, and for doing so with such loving sturdiness. Your confidence gives me courage in this lifelong pursuit of wholeness.

To the Perennial community: your richness of being, creative range, and enduring generosity continue to expand my sense of what it means to show up fully in this shared journey we call life.

To Dee, Joan, Eslinda, Wanjiru, Tatu, Rombo, Randhula, Iromi, Visaka, Abbal, Joshua, Hide, Yuki, Cole, Russ, Neil, Dr. Takekuma, Koichi, Takami, Satoru, Atsuko, Paul, Takeshi, Isao, Douglas, Mark, Brynne, Jon, Tristen, Tru, Mateo, Paxten, and Sayer—thank you for your thoughtful readings, generous feedback, and steadfast support. Your presence in my life story has profoundly shaped this book and continues to be a source of strength and inspiration.

百姓万歳！

ABOUT THE AUTHOR

DR. BRITT YAMAMOTO is an author, entrepreneur, and educator who has spent more than two decades guiding people around the world to live and lead with greater depth, purpose, and presence. A clinical associate professor at the University of Washington and founder of Perennial and RootSpring, he draws on his enduring roots in sustainable agriculture and leadership development to articulate and advance new models of transformation, renewal, and well-being. His first book, *The Soil of Leadership*, is an award-winning international bestseller, translated into multiple languages.

A creature of the Pacific, he is most at home in motion and in stillness—logging long-distance runs, sharing time with his boys, diving beneath ocean swells, flipping through worn vinyl, and following the scent of street food cooked in the open air.